"Sandie Freed is an expe
with years of both drear
book is needed in this season as God increases the dream
releasing to His Body, the Church. Sandie loves the Church and
loves equipping it."

Barbara J. Yoder, lead apostle, Shekinah Regional Apostolic
Center

"Sandie Freed, a prolific author and prophetic voice in the Body
of Christ, shares her personal spiritual journey, the highlights
of which are God-given dreams and visions. In this easy-to-read
volume, Sandie demystifies her subject and shows us how to
practically hear and apply what the Holy Spirit communicates
with us. I highly recommend this book as a manual for spiritual
growth and as a tool to teach others."

Jim Hodges, founder and president, Federation of Ministers
and Churches International

"I have known Sandie Freed for many years, and she is a gifted
writer and an expert in the matters she presents in *Understanding Your Dreams*. As a man who believes God speaks
through dreams, I highly recommend reading this book, and
I believe it will be a valuable resource guide you will want as
part of your permanent library."

Dr. Sanford "Sandy" Kulkin, CEO/founder, The Institute for
Motivational Living

"This book, inspired by the Holy Spirit, unlocks supernatural
revelation in your life. Dr. Sandie Freed is a master communicator, laying a solid biblical foundation to help you understand
your dreams and profoundly transform your life. God wants to
speak to you clearly and powerfully while you sleep, when your
distractions and busyness are dormant. Sleep time is shift time.
Sandie helps you get to know the Master Potter and uncover
the hidden mysteries of God. Let Sandie's teaching, stories and
impartations align your heart, thoughts, life and intentions with
God's eternal plan. Expect the door to revelation to open wide!"

Joseph Peck, M.D., The Time Doctor;
author, *I Was Busy, Now I'm Not*

UNDERSTANDING
YOUR
Dreams

UNDERSTANDING
YOUR
Dreams

HOW TO UNLOCK THE
MEANING OF GOD'S MESSAGES

SANDIE FREED

Chosen

a division of Baker Publishing Group
Minneapolis, Minnesota

Published by Chosen Books
11400 Hampshire Avenue South
Bloomington, Minnesota 55438
www.chosenbooks.com

Chosen Books is a division of
Baker Publishing Group, Grand Rapids, Michigan

Printed in the United States of America

Library of Congress Control Number: 2017946305

ISBN 978-0-8007-9842-0

Cover design by Rob Williams, InsideOutCreativeArts

17 18 19 20 21 22 23   7 6 5 4 3 2 1

I dedicate this book to my husband,
Mickey Freed,
who not only is the love of my life but has
taught me what covenant love truly is. Mickey,
you have always inspired me with your solid
commitment to the Lord, our marriage and
our family. Your steadfastness and dedication
to stand with me, through the good times as
well as the bad times, have empowered me to
find my true north in life. You are an amazing
husband, father and spiritual leader. You are
loved by many—especially by me!

Contents

Foreword

God chooses to communicate with His people through dreams and visions. This form of communication can be misunderstood, dismissed or ignored. Dreams can seem foolish or strange. That is why we need books like *Understanding Your Dreams* by Sandie Freed. This book is awesome!

In both Old and New Covenants, we find many dream scenes and interpretations. The Bible actually has more than fifty references to messages being sent by God through dreams and visions, to the righteous and unrighteous alike. The Lord used dreams and visions in Scripture to guide, warn, direct, help—to communicate His heart.

God has not stopped communicating to humanity by these means. In fact, He often uses dreams and visions to reach unsaved individuals with the Gospel, particularly in closed parts of the world. We hear scores of testimonies of dreams and visions being used by God to draw individuals, families and entire communities to Himself. Similarly, the Lord uses this method of revelation in the lives of most, if not all, believers.

A dream is a release of revelation (whether natural or spiritual) that comes at a time when your body is at peace and you are settled. Sometimes this is the only way God can com-municate with you, because your soul is quiet enough for the Lord to speak deeply into your "spirit man." A dream is like a photograph in movie form of something you are able to relate to. Ecclesiastes 5:3 tells us that "a dream comes when there are many cares."

Dreams are formed in a person's subconscious mind. They are based on the imagery and secret symbolic language that are exclusive and strategic to that person's particular life and destiny. Dreams can be either a subconscious response to the circumstances of our lives or the Holy Spirit communicating His plans, ways and purposes to us. Dreams enable us to tap into the superior ways of the divine Spirit. Dreams enable us to glance into the imperceptible realms of wisdom, counsel, knowledge and might.

The dreams and visions God gives birth to in us bring reve-lation, illumination and inspiration. When we accept delivery of His dream letters of love, God releases the strategic power to change every life event into something wonderful. He turns negative happenings to our advantage and improvement.

In the ancient Eastern world, dreams were treated as reality. Dreams were the world of the divine or the demonic. They often revealed the future. Dreams could be filled with revelation that would cause the dreamer to make the right decision for his or her future.

Once, I was in prayer over a trip to Israel. Barbara Byerly and I were going to be leading prayer for a meeting facilitated by Dr. Peter Wagner that would reconcile Arab Christian leaders and Messianic leaders. Much warfare surrounded this meet-ing. I became very anxious and called Barbara and told her we should pray and fast for three days before going. Barbara was having the same burden and agreed immediately.

In the second day of the fast I fell asleep and had the following dream. Barbara Wentroble, a well-known prophet, was in the dream and asked me a question: "So, you are going to Israel. There are two ways. Which way are you taking?"

I told her the way we were going. In the dream it was as if I was showing her a map and we were wandering through the Arab desert to get to Israel.

"You may go that way," she replied, "but if you do, you will experience much warfare. There is a better way for you to take."

"Oh," I said, "what is that way?"

"Go straight to Israel," she said, "and meet with the leadership you know. Then have your meeting with everyone else."

I woke up and knew that God had spoken to me to give me direction for Dr. Wagner as he proceeded to pull together this meeting. I encouraged him to meet first with the leaders in Israel we knew. Then we could have the overall meeting and reconciliation time.

This proved to be straight revelation from God that affected the overall outcome of our mission.

In the Bible, Israel was forbidden to use many of the same divining practices used by Egypt and other neighboring countries and peoples. Instead, God would visit them in the night to communicate His will and way to them. This continued into the New Covenant. In the first two chapters of the New Testament, God gave direction through prophetic dreams five times.

Sandie Freed is a master of communication, not only with God but also with us. *Understanding Your Dreams* will help you communicate with God about your dreams.

Exercising discernment is very important in determining the source of dreams and visions. We should not ignore what a dream may reveal about our emotions, and we can always ask God to clarify puzzling or disturbing dreams so that He can bring His comfort and healing to our mind, will and emotions. If we discern that a dream is demonic in nature, it might indicate how the enemy is working to thwart us, or it could be a call to a new level of spiritual warfare. All dreams of spiritual origin have some level of significance in our lives, and it is important to invite the Lord into the process of determining the level of significance of each dream. This is why the book you are holding in your hands is so valuable.

Dreams awaken our minds to the unlimited possibilities that await us. This book helps us awaken to the way God communicates. Nothing is impossible when we attach ourselves to the power of His love. Because we are created in God's image, we possess the same power to create through our visual images and words. The dreams we envision grant us agreement with heaven to remove any obstacle that would constrain us to be common.

I highly recommend *Understanding Your Dreams*. We will use it in many of our prophetic seminars. As you read it, expect to find yourself walking and living in a faith realm beyond where you have ever been!

Dr. Chuck D. Pierce, president, Global Spheres, Inc.,
and Glory of Zion International

Acknowledgments

*O*ver fourteen years ago I wrote my first book, *Dream On*. This is a rewrite of that book, and I have learned much concerning dreams and visions since the first publishing of the original. Any new book I write or rewrite requires a new discipline and determination. Each project seems mountainous in proportion. It would be completely ungrateful to reach the top of each mountain and not be thankful for the many friends who helped me reach that summit.

I wish to thank my dad, Bud Davis, for his inspiration to write the original text. Dad, you died before getting to read the final draft and see it published. I know you are reading this in heaven—as you promised me before you died.

To my mom, Deana Davis, thank you for always pushing me to be my best. You were always there to encourage me and never allowed me to settle for less—for anything.

To Pam Garris, my beloved sister, you have *always* been the wind beneath my wings. You believed in me whenever I could not believe in myself. You stood with me during many tough times, and I do mean *tough* times.

To Kim Freed Wheeler, you are still the best thing I ever did. So much of this book involves you, your life and our relationship. Thank you for blessing my life with your life. You have become a beautiful and talented woman. You are anointed of the Lord, and whatever you put your hands to will be successful. I'm so proud of you.

To Pastors Craig and Wendy Bellis, dear friends and colaborers, thank you for being there for me over the past few years. Your prayers have empowered me to make several transitions in my life and have encouraged me to seek more divine truth and biblical understanding of the times in which we live. I just love my Pennsylvania family.

To Paula Bledsoe, my dear friend, intercessor and local editor, we did it again! Thank you for the endless hours of editing each project I endeavor. You are an amazing woman of God. I could not have done this without you.

To the intercessors at Lifegate Church International, thank you for all your support during this season. You are all so amazing, and I value each of you. Your loyalty and love propelled me to finish this project. It is an honor to pastor such special and gifted people.

To Bishop Bill Hamon, my spiritual father for close to thirty years, thank you for believing in me. You took this "Texas Elisha" under your wing and introduced me to a spiritual family that loved me. I'll never forget our times together as we colabored together building the Kingdom of God. You've been my spiritual father, mentor, encourager, and an imparter into my life. It's been a wonderful journey—thank you for being there with me.

To Dr. Jim and Jeanni Davis, my special longtime friends, what would I have done without you? Through the good times and through the bad, at every turn it seems you've been there for me. Without your encouragement, this book never would have been written. Dr. Jim, thank you for all your theological insight into all my books and articles and for taking time to empower me with your wisdom. I love you both dearly.

To the staff at Chosen Books, I want to thank you for being such an anointed and amazing team. Each time I contact anyone at the offices, I am greeted with warmness and genuine love. You *all* go the extra mile with every project, and it shows. Thank you for promoting the Kingdom of God with excellence and integrity.

To Catherine Cooker, my new friend with Chosen Books, thank you for editing the final draft of this book. You truly made my book shine. You are amazing! You made editing smooth and, yes, fun. I so appreciate all of your words of encouragement and prayers as we made this journey together.

To Jane Campbell, editorial director of Chosen Books, thank you for your willingness to read my original proposals concerning dreams and visions and your constant guidance along the way as I climbed another mountain. I am always grateful for opportunities to work with you and Chosen Books. You, dear Jane, are close to my heart, and I know we will be lifelong friends.

1

Meet the Master Potter

*I*f I told you that dreams and visions could utterly transform your life, would you take them more seriously? Would you pay more attention to them? What if I shared that a dream that someone else had about *me* literally saved my life? Or how about this: One night I overdosed on drugs. On the way to the hospital, I had a vision in which the Lord spoke to me very clearly and told me to choose life—and I did! In the vision I knew that if I did not choose life and change, I would die. Dear believer, I am alive today due to many diverse dreams and visions. And I want to share what I believe the Lord desires to do for *you* through them.

First, allow me point out that this book is not simply for giving you more head knowledge concerning this topic. God has much more to give you than just knowledge. Trust me—God desires to meet you face-to-face on this journey! You have an opportunity to know the One who desires to transform, deliver, direct, comfort and empower you through your dreams and visions. Allow me to introduce you to Him as the One who spoke to my young daughter through a dream that saved my life; the One who delivered me through a series of dreams from a virus that almost took my life prematurely; the One who continually speaks to me and gives me godly direction, counsel and confirmation . . . the Master Potter.

You are on a journey to understand the many messages God is sending you—yes, ones that come from your dreams and visions. (I will also refer to them as "spiritual encounters" as we journey together.) You will find that dreams and visions are not unique to us who live today. Spiritual dreams and visions date back centuries and actually have their roots in ancient Judaism. In fact, dreams and visions were the source of major supernatural interventions throughout the history of Judaism and the Church!

Think about that for a moment: God spoke to Abraham through a dream when He established His divine covenant with him and his seed. Eternal covenant promises were given through a dream! A few thousand years later, God did the same thing under the New Covenant: It was through a vision that Peter was instructed to bring the Gospel to the Gentile world. And how about this: God saved the life of His only Son, Jesus Christ, through a series of dreams. Wow! Dreams and visions have their place in history—*His*-story! They have their place in *your story* as well.

It is vitally important for you to have the proper tools to accurately interpret and discern the purpose of your dreams and visions. You now hold a book that will prove helpful on your journey. I have also written chapter 13 to empower you to help your *children* understand their dreams and visions. If you have children of your own or have a ministry to children, you are going to especially love that chapter!

At times on this journey, you will feel as if you are climbing uphill while you are learning the variety of ways to interpret your dreams. Supposedly, climbing uphill is good for us. According to my personal athletic trainer, I *need* to program the "incline" mode on my treadmill because it is healthy for me. Maybe you are a hill climber by profession; maybe you do it to build endurance or to compete athletically. I do not know about you, but I do know that I personally do not like it—at all! I cannot imagine doing it for fun. I mean, really . . . climbing a mountain—for *fun*?

If you are a mountain climber and love it, please do not toss this book across the room! I am simply stating that going uphill takes work, commitment and dedication. My main point is that understanding your dreams and visions will take some effort— but it is well worth it if you will hang in there. A prize awaits you if you will endure this race. Precious believer, you are about to enter into a new level of training. You are being trained to hear heaven's voice and understand heaven's language. As you will read in a bit, heaven's language contains hidden mysteries, and it will require training, commitment, patience and much dedication to understand it.

God is a talking God, and dreams and visions are one way in which He speaks. He has been speaking through such spiritual encounters for centuries, and He still speaks through them. Through dreams and visions He has spoken to both the saved and the unsaved, the righteous and the lost. You have picked up this book because you are interested in understanding heaven's voice expressed through dreams and visions. I assure you—it will greatly benefit you!

Biblical Roots of Dreams and Visions

I have good news for you: You are in good hands, for God has been speaking to mankind for centuries through spiritual encounters. Let's take a moment and consider the biblical foundation for dreams and visions. More than one third of the Bible relates to dreams and visions, and in more than fifty references to them, God delivered divine messages through them. Some examples:

- One of the first dreams documented in Scripture was given to King Abimelech as a warning concerning Sarah, Abraham's wife (Genesis 20:3).

- It was during Abraham's dream that God made a covenant with him and his descendants (Genesis 15:12–18).

- Through dreams, Jacob received God's promise regarding his heritage (Genesis 31:10–13).

- God revealed Joseph's destiny through dreams (Genesis 37:5–11; 19–20). Later Joseph interpreted Pharaoh's dreams (Genesis 41:1–8, 15–16, 25–32).

- Joseph, the husband of Mary, was also a dreamer. The angel of the Lord appeared to him in a dream with instructions to take Mary, though pregnant, as his wife (Matthew 1:20–21). After Herod's death, the angel of the Lord appeared to Joseph again in a dream to direct him where to take Jesus (Matthew 2:19–20).

- Gideon overcame his fear and inferiority complex and became a mighty warrior because of a dream (Judges 7:13–15).

- Daniel had the gift to interpret dreams for King Nebuchadnezzar (Daniel 2:26–28).

- Ezekiel records four visions (though he recorded no dreams).

- The prophet Isaiah witnessed the throne room of God through a vision (Isaiah 6). He described what we understand today as an apostolic sending: "Here am I, Lord, send me!" (see verse 8).

- Jeremiah had a vision of God "touching" his mouth and appointing him to carry God's word (Jeremiah 1:9).

- The New Testament begins with five dreams and three visions.

- The Bible ends with the book of Revelation, which documents incredible visions over 22 chapters.

These examples reveal that God definitely speaks through dreams and visions. He is a supernatural God who spoke to His people through supernatural encounters. We must also note, however, that the supernatural encounters described above include multitudes of symbols and mysteries. I will explain more about the reason for the hidden "mysteries" of God and His heavenly language of symbolism in chapter 4. For now, you may feel that learning the symbolism of heaven is an uphill battle. Be patient—building your own personal dream vocabulary and developing interpretation will take time, patience and, yes . . . endurance!

Always keep this thought in the back of your mind: God loves you and His heart is to draw you continually nearer to Him. He will reveal many mysteries through your dreams to keep drawing you nearer to Him so that you may know Him.

It is through dreams and visions that God communicates with us concerning our futures and our destinies. He also reveals the destinies of our mates, families, workplaces and nations. In the first few chapters of this book, I will help you build a foundation that will empower you to understand the Master's hand and His plans as developed and revealed in your dream life. You will learn that some of your dreams are warning dreams. Some are directional. Others require an immediate response and prayer. On this journey you will discover various categories of dreams. Unless we can first wake up and write down our dreams, however, they might be completely lost.

This book is a guide to understanding your dreams and visions—what they are and what to do with them. It will empower you to understand the diversity of dream symbolism and aid you in interpreting your dreams. Dreamer, you have dreams from God, and He has given them for a purpose. We are here to find out why He gives them.

Now, expect the door to revelation concerning your dreams and visions to open wide!

The Master's Hand

I have been studying dreams and visions for more than thirty years, and I have learned that God uses them to mold and shape my life. Whenever I think about dreams and visions, I am reminded that His main purpose is always to draw us nearer to Him and to continue an intimate relationship with each of us. He also speaks often in dreams and visions, however, to give me direction, edification, comfort and, yes, correction.

Since He is a good God—always!—I am continually reminded of His handiwork in my life. Like a weaver of beautiful tapestry, He has woven many different events (some good, some bad with good endings!) into the tapestry of my life story. He is truly a master weaver. I love what James W. and Michal Ann Goll have to say in their insightful book, *Dream Language*: "As the Master Weaver, God is weaving the renowned tapestry of human history; He is interlacing the warp and weft of each of our individual lives into the pattern of His own design."[1] It is very true—only the Lord can make all things work together for good . . . and actually make them come out looking desirable (see Romans 8:28–29).

In Scripture God is identified as Emmanuel, "God with us"; Yahweh, who introduced Himself not only as "I am" but who "I will be"—the God of covenant; and El Shaddai, the "all-sufficient One." In my dreams, He has often presented Himself as Jehovah Rapha, "the God that heals." He is described as the Rock, the Vine, the Good Shepherd, the Lamb and the Door. All of these names and symbols describe Him, and you will discover many others that He uses to identify Himself through dreams and visions.

Many of my dreams have revealed God to be "the Lord who molds me," which always reminds me of the Master Potter to whom the prophet Jeremiah related (see Jeremiah 18:6). This idea comes from the Hebrew name Jehovah Makkeh, which means "the Lord our smiter."[2] As imperfect humans, we can easily mistake our heavenly Father for a vengeful God who stands ready with His whip to smite us for every sin. But, in fact, Isaiah 53:4–5 reminds us that God smote *Jesus* instead with our sins, griefs, sorrows and even sickness so that we would not have to be smitten with them. What Jesus accomplished on the cross allows us to be corrected and receive the miracle of being molded into His divine image through God's love and forgiveness. When He sees something that needs adjustment, He does what any potter would: He places us on His wheel and uses it to correct us.

I met the Master Potter in Sunday school at the age of eleven. I walked the aisle to receive Him as my Savior. But it was not until later in life that I really understood Him as the One who molded my life. I met that person the day I sat in front of a minister with his potter's wheel. He held a lump of lifeless clay before my eyes and explained that this is what I was in the hands of the Lord—nothing without Him! I watched as he molded that lump of nothingness and made it into something beautiful. I observed his hands carefully fashioning the clay until it became both beautiful and useful. I was in awe! It was as if the Lord Himself was standing in front of me, talking straight to me: *Sandie, let Me have your life—I can make your life beautiful. I am all you need.* I was in terrible pain at that time in my life, and I needed to know Him as the Potter. I needed His hand to fashion and mold me. Yes, I truly met Him that day—I rededicated my life to Him—and He has continued to shape my life through many heavenly encounters, including dreams and visions.

Jeremiah's Vision of the Potter's Wheel

Let's look more closely at the passage where the Lord uses a potter at his wheel to depict Himself as the Potter and mankind as a vessel being molded by His hand. As you read, I am certain that your heart will be softened as mine is each time I meditate on this passage. After all, He has been reshaping and molding each of us—especially through His messages revealed in dreams and visions—with the intent of . . . *shaping us as it seems best to Him!* It is time to grab a pencil, pen or highlighter. You will want to underline every place in this book where you know that the Holy Spirit is sparking your heart! I italicize the words in this passage for a reason: It is important to understand the heart of God as He molds, shapes and forms us through dreams and visions.

> This is the word that came to Jeremiah from the LORD: "Go down to the *potter's house*, and there I will give you my *message*." So I went down to the potter's house, and I saw him working at the wheel. But the pot he was *shaping* from the clay was *marred* in his hands; so the potter *formed* it into another pot, *shaping it as seemed best to him.*
>
> Then the word of the LORD came to me: *"O house of Israel, can I not do with you as this potter does?"* declares the LORD. *"Like clay in the hand of the potter, so are you in my hand*, O house of Israel."
>
> Jeremiah 18:1–6, emphasis added

In biblical times, craftsman potters were quite common. The making of pottery ranks among the most ancient of crafts, and over time the shaping of different vessels became very well developed. Vessels before 1500 BC were fashioned by hand and irregularly shaped; only after this time did potters' wheels become widely used, and the clay itself was of finer quality and fired with much more intense heat. The wares were thinner, lighter and more decorative. Jeremiah, who prophesied from 626 BC to 586 BC, observed a cultivated artisan's craft.

Can you envision what Jeremiah saw when he found the potter's house? He probably noticed nearby clay fields that the potter frequented to find his clay. When he entered the potter's work area, Jeremiah would have also found a kiln in which to fire the clay, the potter's wheel and a nearby dump where unusable clay and fragments were placed.

Imagine God speaking to Jeremiah as he observed the potter. The craftsman took a lump of clay and placed it on the wheel next to which he sat and shaped the clay with his hands. This was not, by the way, ordinary clay—it was a special mixture of clay from the earth that was trodden by men's feet, forming it into a paste. I believe this is symbolic of the way the Lord uses experiences in which we have been trampled down, leading to hardened hearts or flawed lives. He takes those broken-down areas and remolds us into a beautiful masterpiece reflecting His love, care and glory.

The wheel, consisting of a wooden disk placed on top of a larger one, was turned by an attendant or through a treadle (a pedal or lever operated by the foot to spin the wheel). When the clay was perfectly formed, it was smoothed and coated with a glaze before finally being fired in a furnace. If, during the process of being shaped on the wheel, the clay became stiff, or if the potter found a small stone, it had now become marred and had to be reshaped and molded into a different vessel . . . one pleasing to the potter.

The Jewish potters formed many different types of vessels, and what I find extremely interesting is that Jewish wares had a "Jewish stamp" or a "type ore" on them. I suppose you might liken it to an artist signing his name somewhere on the canvas of his masterpiece. When God had Jeremiah watch the potter shape the clay, He was signifying that His signature would be on the finished piece. All the while we are documenting our dreams and visions and praying over the interpretations, God is shaping our future through them and applying His personal signature to each part of our lives! The potter's total control over the clay in Jeremiah's passage is likened to God's complete control over mankind.

The message of the potter and the clay is one that has always been dear to my heart. I continually desire to be good soil, or clay, with which God is pleased. I attempt to remain pliable in His hands. I desperately desire that He mold me and make me fit for His use. And yet . . . I mess up! I hate to admit it, but I do.

You will find that I am fairly transparent when I write or teach, but I do not enjoy transparency at times. In this book, you will read about my desperate need for a forgiving and loving God and how I *know* He has had to take my lump of clay and redo it. You will read about the times when I was at death's door because of an eating disorder, and how my life was saved by a dream that God gave to my daughter. You will also read how the Lord revealed generational curses through a series of dreams and visions—another intervention that saved my life from destruction. Dreams and visions have truly saved my life! Yes, I am Sandie *Freed*—one who is now delivered and *freed up* to walk in freedom—because of dreams and visions.

God is continually reshaping my life. I have made wrong turns, taken detours that led to nowhere and at times made ridiculous decisions. Still He would faithfully pick me up and place me back on the wheel. Round and round I would go, being reshaped. And, dear one, I can testify that God has used dreams and visions as part of my reshaping process.

As I stated earlier, God uses spiritual encounters to encourage me, direct me and instruct me . . . but also to correct me. The Potter's hand has had to be firm at times—especially when I am stiff-necked and hardheaded. Just as clay had to be reworked and refashioned if it became too stiff, it is the same with us. Many times we stiffen up and become unteachable. (I guess God might call that "stiff-necked"!) It is in these types of situations that God will bypass the mind and speak straight to our spirits in a dream or vision.

Works of His Hands

David knew God as one who promised to create continually a clean heart. God promises to do the same for us. The psalmists write about the works of God's hands, how He formed the world and also mankind:

> The heavens are telling of the glory of God; and their expanse is declaring the *work of His hands.*
>
> Psalm 19:1 NASB, emphasis added

> When I consider Your heavens, the *work of Your fingers*, the moon and the stars, which You have ordained, what is man that You are mindful of him, and the son of man that You visit him?
>
> Psalm 8:3–4 NKJV, emphasis added

> For Thou didst form my inward parts; Thou didst weave me in my mother's womb. I will give thanks to Thee, for I am fearfully and wonderfully made.
>
> Psalm 139:13–14 NASB 1977

Yes, He is the Master Potter. He forms, shapes and fashions us to be instruments of righteousness—used for His glory. He weaves the tapestry of human history and uses everything to bring Him glory. *And much of the shaping, forming and weaving is done through divine encounters from heaven—especially in dreams and visions.* Keep this in mind: God deals with someone until *He* wins! Just as God dealt with Moses in the wilderness, David in the cave, Paul on his donkey, Peter and his hardheadedness concerning the Gentiles—He will deal with us through dreams and visions until He gets His way, because He loves us. He is never *not* pursuing us! Even in our sleep He is actively pursuing intimacy with us—pursuing our hearts.

"Your hands have made me, cunningly *fashioned* and established me; give me understanding, that I may learn Your

29

commandments" (Psalm 119:73 AMPC, emphasis added). Just as God molds us, He is also fashioning us. King David understood that it was God who fashioned him. The Hebrew word for "fashioned" in Psalm 119:73 implies that God prepares us, frames our lives and desires that we be perfected. When I study how David described God's desire to perfect him, I believe it is safe to say that when we are in His hands, He also desires for us to experience change that is divine transformation.

Dreams and Visions Transform Our Lives

Dreams and visions are tools that release transformation. Romans 12:2 instructs us, "Do not conform any longer to the pattern of this world, but be *transformed* by the renewing of your mind. Then you will be able to test and approve what God's will is—his good, pleasing and perfect will" (emphasis added). Dreams and visions are given many times as methods of renewing our minds. Transformation always begins from the inside out. Therefore, God will speak to your innermost being through dreams and visions to transform your life. Dear one, let me assure you that if you go through a season when you turn from God and become more conformed to the world, then God will most likely come crashing through your dream world and speak to you concerning the need for transformation. He speaks to us about changing into His image in many different ways, and dreams and visions are definitely avenues. Remember, the Master Potter is committed to taking a marred vessel and re-forming it. He never gives up on us—and I am glad!

Transformation always involves change. In fact, the Greek word for transformation is *metamorphoo*, which reminds us of a caterpillar changing into a butterfly. We are being changed into His image through the process of *metamorphoo* (transformation).

I remember studying butterflies when I attended elementary school. We observed the caterpillar inching its way through life only to find itself in the dark surroundings of a chrysalis. The worm dies but the creature is still alive, undergoing a re-forming process that reconstructs its image. Everything but a handful of cells that will form each organ is broken down and re-formed. After a few more weeks of isolation, suddenly a breakthrough occurs. Transformation and change have taken place, and it is time for the release of a new life. That which was once a worm is now a lovely creature . . . the butterfly!

Each of God's children undergoes an identical process. As I stated earlier, we are transformed from the inside out, much like the butterfly. When we receive Jesus as our Lord and Savior, we are born again, but we still have many obstacles to overcome. Being born again assures us of our salvation and eternal life. It does not, however, immediately deliver us from future problems, impure thought patterns or mindsets of the old life. Upon our salvation and with our obedience, His plans for transformation begin to unfold, and the Master Physician begins His intricate work. I visualize this transformation as a process similar to cosmetic surgery, transforming us into His image. Cutting here and there and perfecting are all part of this surgery.

We often find ourselves in the wilderness during these times— in our own chrysalis. It is a dark, lonely and sometimes very secluded place to be while He works on every part of our being. At times, we feel as if we are going to die! In fact, we *do* die . . . to self and selfish ambition. But once His work is completed, we rise up and fly. Similar to the butterfly, we are now changed, feeling exhilarated with our new freedom. This is what the Lord has planned for each of us: freedom in Christ. He whom the Son sets free is free indeed (see John 8:36). And, precious reader, this book is all about each of us experiencing freedom in Christ, through the revelation given in dreams and visions!

I have written this book because I want you to gain the benefit from all I have experienced and learned about the power of dreams and visions. My life testifies that dreams and visions are tools for transformation. God is continually moving us to higher levels of understanding the mysteries of heaven, which involve understanding dreams and visions, as well as transforming us more into His divine image. As the Master Potter, He remakes and remolds us, and He will use dreams and visions as part of His plan for reconstruction. The dreams God gives will motivate you to change, to rise up and be all He has destined you to become. The dreams He releases will lead you to paths promising revealed truth, freedom and deliverance. King David understood the importance of the Master Potter actually "fashioning" or molding him for the purpose of knowing God and His ways.

Believer, it is the same with each of us. He molds our lives and fashions us according to His purposes. The process of transformation involves not only change but also being "fashioned" according to His perfect will and directives for our lives. Dreams and visions are tools that He uses to fashion and transform us!

New Age versus the Prophetic

I would be remiss if I did not mention that many non-Christian books have attempted to guide others in interpreting their dreams and visions. These books, however, are *not* inspired by the Holy Spirit. The New Age movement unfortunately promotes the use of fortune-tellers, spirit guides and, yes, demonic involvement when interpreting dreams.

Many people today, especially in Western culture, rely on natural understanding rather than divine intervention and revelation when considering dreams and visions. Many do not believe that God desires to speak to them, and they remain skeptical about hearing the voice of God. Allow me to take some time to explain your spiritual heritage in hearing God's voice. You are part of a prophetic generation that has been anointed to know His voice more intimately than generations that came before.

According to Ephesians 4:11, God has ordained the five-fold ministry offices of apostle, prophet, evangelist, pastor and teacher. Over the last several years, the Lord has been restoring each of these offices to the Church. The prophet and the apostle are now being reestablished; the prophets gained their beachhead in the 1990s, while apostles have been coming to the forefront in the 21st century.

As the prophets began to arise, there was a noticeable release of the prophetic voice. This voice has been penetrating the earth with audible revelations of God's perfect will through corporate and personal prophecy. *At the same time, God began to speak more profoundly through dreams and visions.* By closely examining Joel 2:28, we understand that in the end times God will pour out His Spirit on all flesh, and there will be an increase of dreams and visions: "And it shall come to pass afterward that I will pour out My Spirit on all flesh; your sons and your daughters shall prophesy, your old men shall dream dreams, your young men shall see visions" (Joel 2:28 NKJV).

Being a Prophetic People

It is clear in this passage that dreams and visions are a manifestation of the prophetic movement that is still occurring. Part of this divine move of God involves becoming a prophetic people. Some have concluded that in order to be prophetic in gifting, they must be called to be prophets. Not at all. Let me attempt to again clarify this misconception by explaining the functions of a prophetic people.

First, not all have to become prophets to be prophetic people. Prophetic people are simply those who hear God's voice, know His voice and move by His voice. So be encouraged! This means that we can all have a prophetic ear to hear His voice. In the Old Testament, a prophet was referred to as a "seer." Today, God is raising up many who are gifted to see into many realms of the Spirit and experience supernatural encounters. Precious reader, I believe that, as you read this book, the "seer" in you will be activated. Expect it!

When the prophetic voice is released, things begin to happen. When God releases His prophetic voice through a dream or vision, things begin to happen as well! Ezekiel 37:3–10 tells the story of the prophet Ezekiel, who was taken in a vision to a valley filled with dry bones. When he began to prophesy to the dry bones, he heard a noise and a shaking. Bones began to come alive. A graveyard of dead, dry bones began to move and come together, forming a great army. The prophetic movement continues to release the same type of sound! Things are continuing to shake and move; we are experiencing a shift in the heavenlies. *Webster's Dictionary* defines a shift as "moving from one place to another." When something begins to shift, things begin to change. When the prophetic voice is released, whether through a declaration or a dream or a vision, God's perfect will is established, and things begin to change and move!

Impartations from Heaven

If you understand the language of heaven, you notice that it is God's will to release an impartation with the revelation. During a dream encounter, God can impart to your spirit. A biblical example is when God imparted divine wisdom to Solomon as he was dreaming (see 1 Kings 3).

The word *impart* can be found in several Scriptures; my favorite, and, I believe, the one that best explains what I am attempting to convey, is Romans 1:11–12 (AMPC):

> For I am yearning to see you, that I may impart and share with you some spiritual gift to strengthen and establish you; that is, that we may be mutually strengthened and encouraged and comforted by each other's faith, both yours and mine.

34

The word translated "impart" in this passage is the Greek word *metadidomi*, meaning "to give over"—as if to share. Therefore, we can view an impartation as a "giving over" of what I desire to share with you—the revelation I have received. Wisdom and understanding of dreams and visions are being imparted to you as you read . . . believe it and receive it! I will continue to impart as I write; hang in there with me—you are being transformed (changed) as we journey together!

Throughout this book I will continue to give testimony of what the Lord has done in my life. I love to give Him glory continually; He has always remained faithful to give me what is needed to live a victorious life. I have realized that when you open your spirit to prophetic revelation, you begin to change. The book of Samuel gives a clear illustration of how the prophetic anointing affected Saul's life. In 1 Samuel 10:5–6, notice how Scripture defines the transforming impact of the prophetic anointing upon Saul. The power of the prophetic mantle changed Saul into a different person:

> And the Spirit of the LORD will come upon thee, and thou shalt prophesy with them, and shalt be turned into another man. . . . And it was so, that when he had turned his back to go from Samuel, God gave him another heart: and all those signs came to pass that day.
>
> 1 Samuel 10:6, 9 KJV

Therefore, since dreams are part of the prophetic movement, expect God to speak to you in the night seasons. He will begin to communicate His will because God desires for all to be changed into His image. The Word says that we *move* from faith to faith, from strength to strength and from glory to glory.

> They go from strength to strength, every one of them in Zion appeareth before God.
>
> Psalm 84:7 KJV

For therein is the righteousness of God revealed from faith to faith: as it is written, the just shall live by faith.

Romans 1:17 KJV

But we all, with open face beholding as in a glass the glory of the Lord, are changed into the same image from glory to glory, even as by the Spirit of the Lord.

2 Corinthians 3:18 KJV

Notice that we are to *move*! In moving will come the changing. You will begin to realize that God will use dreams to purify your heart and to release new levels of transformation.

You Are in Good Hands!

Believer, you are in the Potter's hand now. As you continue to read, expect to feel His touch! And remember . . . as you dream, He is shaping your life and your future. You are on a journey of transformation, impartation and continual divine intervention. I just know that you are ready for change. You are reading this book because you truly desire to hear God's voice and understand heaven's language spoken through your dreams and visions. You will not be disappointed! God has you in His hands, molding, shaping, fashioning and breathing life into you now!

2

God Is a Talking God

I could barely move as the other people in the room lifted their voices to the old Baptist hymn. My lips quivered, some of the words falling out as I tried to sing. "All to Jesus, I surrender; all to Him I freely give. I surrender all . . ."

Ugh! I did not want to sing that day. I did not want to be in Sunday school. The thought raced through my mind as the pianist kept playing the song: *Sandie, you shouldn't be here! You should be dead!*

If I had had my way, I would have died the night before. That is right—on Saturday night I had attempted suicide. In desperation, feeling extremely rejected by my classmates, I grabbed a bottle of aspirin. It was completely full, containing more than 250 tablets. Hoping no one would suspect, I raced to my room, concealing the bottle underneath my floor-length robe. I grabbed a glass of water that was by the bathroom sink. With tears flowing, I began to guzzle handfuls of aspirin. Becoming more and more nauseated with each swallow, I forced myself to keep each tablet down.

I knew I needed help, but I did not know how to get it. I needed deliverance, but I did not know what deliverance was. Since I had been a young child, all I had known was torment. Nightmares plagued my childhood sleep, and dark visions tormented me; yet no one knew how to help me, empower me through them or even stop to pray for me. My family was from a denominational background and did not understand the power of dreams and visions from the spiritual realm, especially those of a demonic nature. Bottom line, I was now sixteen years old and had never understood that God wanted to communicate with me.

I wish I had known that God desired to visit me in the night seasons. I did not believe that God even cared about me. I was in so much emotional pain that the only way out seemed to be death.

Obviously, I wanted to escape—to heaven, I hoped. My last thoughts that night were filled with rejection, shame, fears of abandonment and tremendous emotional pain. *These pills will solve everything,* I thought to myself. *I will never feel pain again!* My tears became a river, and yet the pain began to lift as my mind floated into a place where only dreams and deep sleep occur.

Allowed to Live for a Purpose

I awakened on Sunday morning to Mom's voice. "Sandie, you'll be late for Sunday school!"

Wait a minute! I thought. *I'm dead! Is Mom with me in heaven?* I looked around groggily, trying to overcome the fog of sleep. *Where is God? I thought I was supposed to meet Him! Surely there is no Sunday school in heaven.*

Once again, Mom pounded on my bedroom door and expressed the need to "get it in gear." "You're going to be late!"

Was I mad! Not because I had to go to Sunday school, but because I did not die! *I can't even kill myself well!* I scolded inwardly—it was merely affirmation that I could never do anything right. All those pills . . . and *still* I was alive. Anger and hostility arose in me with each breath. I was angry with God, because I knew that He had intervened—but why? I was a bad person; how could God not know that? Why would He not just let me die?

I struggled getting dressed. I did not respond to my mother's haste; I could not. I was sluggish from the effects of the aspirin.

In Sunday school, the song finally finished. I ended the last chorus with my friends, and we waited for our teacher to begin the Sunday school lesson. Amazingly, it was a message of God's endless love and grace. I will never forget that day. The teacher confirmed God's forgiveness for all our sins. But as she spoke, my mind kept wandering off. *I wish I could be happy. I want to be free! I'm saved, but I still don't know God.*

Then, out of the thoughts echoing in my mind, I heard her say something startling: "My sheep listen to my voice," she quoted from John 10:27–28. "I know them, and they follow me. I give them eternal life, and they shall never perish; no one can snatch them out of my hand."

That got my attention. God had snatched me from the jaws of death! But why? How could He love me or care enough for me that He would give me my life back? I felt such shame, and yet the Bible had promised that Jesus' followers could hear His voice. *What?* I thought to myself. *How can I do that?* I desperately cried out to hear Him in a more intimate way. Somewhere inside of me I understood that God loved me so much that He gave me a second chance. It was one of the moments that turned my life around. Knowing I could hear His voice, that He loved me, that He obviously had a destiny for me to fulfill empowered me that day to move forward in life and seek Him more. I never attempted suicide again, though, as you will read later, I still had a death wish that needed to be broken off.

At sixteen years old I was just beginning a journey toward complete deliverance and freedom. It took years for me to realize that I could train myself to hear His voice and, more importantly, that God really wanted me to hear Him. He *desired* to talk to me! As it turns out, dreams and visions were the tools God used for that deliverance and emotional healing. Just as He watched over me that day, God knows right where you are *today*! He knows your past and your future. He will use dreams and visions, just as He has done for Sandie Freed, to lead you into divine fulfillment!

God *Really* Wants to Talk to You!

Precious one, God *really* wants to talk to you! He wants to communicate with each of us. Years ago I did not realize this; I attended a denominational church where the gifts of the Spirit were not taught and revelation from the Lord was not understood or sought. My parents were uneducated concerning the importance of dreams, so I was never taught to pay attention to them.

Besides that, for years I considered myself unworthy and believed that God would not waste His time with a wretched sinner like myself. After all, God only spoke to really "spiritual people" who had it all together . . . preachers, teachers and pastors, right? Terms such as *anointing*, *deliverance* and *breakthrough* were foreign to me.

Often I would channel surf the television and stop to view a "faith minister" who proclaimed that God spoke to him. I would question their messages of faith because they announced that "God told me" or "The Lord spoke to me." My response was to think that these people were nuts! I did not believe that God would speak to people. He was on His throne, and He had no time to mess with us on the earth. (Well, with the exception of speaking to Moses from the burning bush.) Then I would announce that there was another fruit loop on television! Yet something deep inside me hungered to hear from God. I wanted desperately to hear His voice, but it seemed impossible. God would never do those things for me, would He?

Only later in life did I realize that God does indeed desire to speak to us. Not to just a select few, but to all! As I mentioned earlier, God wants each of us to know Him and how much He loves us. Think of dreams and visions as God's love language! I also discovered that dreams and visions are part of His plan to fully restore His people. I wrote my testimony in this chapter so that you can see how God spared my life for a purpose. As you will read later, the Lord gave me dreams and visions that revealed why I tried to take my life at the age of sixteen. At the time I attempted suicide, all I understood was pain. Now I know differently. Dreams and visions were given to me by God so that I could avoid the desire for premature death that haunted me for years. God has an eternal purpose for dreams and visions, and I want to share my many victories with you. Keep reading—there is hope for you, also!

Receivers of Dreams and Visions

From the beginning, God brought dreams, visions and heavenly encounters into existence to convey messages to His people. As a supernatural God, He communicates with us in supernatural ways. Angels, for example, are documented in Scripture from the book of Genesis forward. And the words *dream* or *vision* and their variations occur more than two hundred times in the Bible, starting with Genesis.

Throughout biblical history, we read how God used dreams to speak to His people. In Old Testament times, dream language was one of His most prominent ways of communicating. In Numbers 12:6 we see God's intent to make Himself known to

His children through dreams and visions: "When a prophet of the LORD is among you, I reveal myself to him in visions, I speak to him in dreams" (Numbers 12:6). God Himself was explaining the subtle differences between dreams and visions in this verse: By saying, "I speak to him," He is speaking about a deep relationship or intimacy, but when He says, "I reveal myself," it speaks of showing God's divine nature or His attributes. When we dream, it is God's intent for us to connect our hearts with His. In a vision, however, His nature is being revealed. No wonder God has heavenly encounters planned for us. He wants to show us His glory and also empower us to understand His heart. Wow!

Most of the time, God's purpose in a vision is to reveal His nature, while dreams are more often given for direction or to show His divine plan for our lives. Numbers 12:6 allows us to recognize God's interaction with His people—directing them through their daily lives as well as proving Himself to them as the almighty God.

God gave dreams to Abraham (whom God also refers to as a prophet in Genesis 20:7) concerning four centuries of slavery in Egypt, showing that his descendants would endure and be given deliverance from their captivity (see Genesis 15:12–14). Jacob, Abraham's grandson, received a dream during a time when he was running away from home to save his own life (see Genesis 28:10–22). While he was fleeing, darkness set in and Jacob had to bed down for the night—using a hard rock for a pillow. That night he dreamed of a ladder reaching from earth to heaven, with angels ascending and descending. At the top of the ladder, Jacob beheld God. Jacob considered this dream a divine encounter, so upon awakening he took the stone he used as his pillow and made it a "pillar of remembrance" of the day he met God. Then, he poured oil on it as an act of worship. We know that the rock symbolizes Christ the Rock, the Chief Cornerstone of Jacob's life and our lives today! My question

42

to you is this: Will you treat each dream as an encounter and then act on it with holy worship? I pray that we all take our dreams more seriously.

Daniel was another who both received and interpreted dreams. Take some time and read through Daniel 7, in which he records his prophetic dreams. How about Joseph? Genesis 37:1–11 relates his dreams of his brothers and his father bowing down to him. Yet it was twenty years before Joseph would witness their fulfillment. Interestingly, Joseph was not only a dreamer but also a dream interpreter. While in prison, he was given an opportunity to interpret the dreams of Pharaoh's butler and baker. The interpretations God gave Joseph opened the door for him to be promoted to the position of prime minister in Egypt.

Then there is Solomon, the wisest person ever to have lived, who received an impartation in a divine dream (see 1 Kings 3:5–14). The Lord invited Solomon to ask for whatever he desired, and Solomon asked for wisdom so that he might be a good ruler over his people. God was so pleased with Solomon's request that He gave him not only wisdom but much, much more—including great wealth! I love the fact that Solomon's dream includes an impartation—for we can receive an impartation from a dream or a vision, as I mentioned in chapter 1—but I also love that Solomon's dream involved interactivity. Many times God will interact with us through our dreams.

The New Testament continues with many examples of dreams given to believers, such as Joseph, Mary's husband, who had a dream about where to move Jesus for protection (see Matthew 2:13). Yes, the Father saved His own Son, Jesus Christ, through dreams! And then there is the dream received by the apostle Paul, in which a man from Macedonia was calling to him for help (see Acts 16:9). This dream led to the Gospel of Christ being introduced to the European continent.

Defining Dreams

The Hebraic language makes little distinction between dreams and visions. Although there are specific occasions in which the Bible makes a clear distinction between the two, numerous times Scripture leaves us somewhat confused as to whether someone had a dream or a vision. The main idea in both experiences is that the reality behind the supernatural occurrence is the same. In other words, they are equally important. Regardless if it was man talking to God; God talking to man; man seeing, hearing or talking with angels; or man receiving prophecy, dreams or visions—it was all considered a supernatural encounter. And it is all deemed just as important in the New Testament.

Even today, the Jews place importance on dreams and visions and their interpretations. Many Jews still abide by the ancient practice of training their children to honor these supernatural encounters and to continually prepare their hearts for divine visitations. The children are also encouraged to keep a type of dream journal so that they can continually reflect on God and His directives.

I am a strong encourager of preparing our hearts for divine encounters during the night and documenting each dream, vision or supernatural encounter. For us today I want to stress the need to journal our dreams. After all, this is a way that we write the vision and make it plain, as instructed in Habakkuk 2:2.

So . . . what exactly is a dream? For the most part, dreams are a series of thought images or emotions that occur during one's sleep. Daniel referred to dreams as "visions of his head upon his bed" (Daniel 7:1 KJV), and they have also been referred to as "night visions." Many times Scripture records that the Lord visited people "in the night season," which represents a dream.

A dream is often likened to a story that a person simply watches while sleeping. Dreams given to us by God are in the form of parabolic language and are almost always symbolic.

When I began to document my dreams, the different scenes did not appear to connect. The story seemed to jump from here to there. I have learned through experience to simply document the symbolism, and through time and patience the Lord will direct the interpretation. I also have learned to be patient, not allowing discouragement to hinder the full interpretation. Remember, God is in control. And He will be faithful to guide you in the full revelation of your dreams.

Dreams from God come in the same language as the parables He told on earth, like illustrated stories. Sometimes they are clear and straightforward, but most of the time they are symbolic, and, therefore, need interpretation. Since they are parabolic in nature, as with the parables of Jesus, the true meaning of the dream is often hidden.

I have found that true dreams that are sent from God come in the form of metaphors, similes, poems, parabolic illustrations, rhymes, riddles and incredible story lines. It is safe to say that dreams mainly occur while asleep and visions mostly occur while awake; I have, however, had a vision in which I was dreaming a dream. After gaining my natural senses, I realized I had a dream while also experiencing a vision! So I like to say concerning dreams and visions, "Nothing is always!" God can do what He desires and when He desires.

When Solomon received the impartation of wisdom in a dream, God was interacting with him in a process called "lucid dreaming." Not only does He speak to us, He is also expecting a response! Once we know and understand this, we will begin to act on it. There have been times while dreaming that I literally asked the Lord if we could talk about the dream and change it! In these cases the dreams needed to be "flipped" to have a different outcome. Usually I needed to repent of something in the dream, and after repentance the outcome would change. God loves this sort of interaction—not because He does not already know the outcome, but because it is yet another opportunity for us to develop more intimacy with Him.

Dreams are also not limited to the night season. I have had many experiences when I was praying about a situation and fell asleep, and God gave me the answer to my questions in a dream! He bypasses our minds and puts us to sleep so that our natural understanding does not hinder what needs to be received in the spirit. While we are still, we can more easily listen to the Lord.

Sleep Time Is Shift Time

Scientists have documented dreams as a product of brain activity that occurs during REM, or rapid eye movement. The REM stage of sleep must be experienced in order for dreams to occur. Many nights I have felt as if I dreamed all night long, but the more likely explanation is that only one dream occurred during the REM cycle. I have also learned, however, that I cannot limit the supernatural intervention of the Holy Spirit, who is in total control of time. Establishing how long I sleep, how long my dream was or how many dreams I can experience is irrelevant. It is more important to focus on the *dream itself* and not scientific applications that will limit our interpretations.

Most adults dream three to five times during an average sleep of eight hours. You may have three or more dreams, but you may only remember one. Sometimes you might remember three or more. By journaling the different scenes and settings, you will be able to determine if the dreams are connected and have a common theme. I will provide ideas for dream documentation in chapter 8, but for now I want you to think of dreams as personalized encoded messages from heaven . . . God is talking to you!

One third of our lifetime involves sleeping. This is based on a normal twenty-four-hour day in which we are awake for sixteen hours and get eight hours of sleep. But let it sink in a different way: If approximately one third of our lives are spent sleeping, that is one third of our lives that God can interject His thoughts and directives straight to our spirits! Over the course of our lifetimes, we will have spent thousands of hours dreaming; scientists estimate as many as *eight years* of our lives are wrapped up in dreams. That time is accountable to God—and if He is speaking, I want to know. I want every minute of those eight years for growing in God and moving forward into destiny. How about you?

Eight hours of sleep per night, eight years of our lives spent dreaming . . . These eights are important, for the number eight in the Bible represents new beginnings. Believer, based on these facts, each morning you awake, you can have a new beginning, a fresh start—to begin a "new thing" with God. Yes, use these dream times as opportunities to remind yourself that the old has passed away and that all things (in you and through you) are becoming new! A dream can give fresh opportunity to take off the old man and put on the new (see Ephesians 4:22–24). After dreams, when God speaks to your heart, you can rise up and declare, "I am no longer subject to the temptations or directions of the old sin nature; now I am alive to the new. I am a new creation!" Take a moment for this to sink in. Grab your highlighter and mark this section *Important.* Dog-ear the page if needed so that you never take dream time for granted again. You have an opportunity to shift into fulfilling destiny every time you dream. Take advantage of it!

Determining Visions

Visions are similar to dreams and can occur during the day or night, but usually when we are awake. It is as if God opens our spiritual eyes to see what is actually taking place in the spiritual realm. The Hebrew offers a simpler definition, documenting visions as "a revelation." Visions release revelation about what is *real* in the supernatural!

Sometimes it is difficult to determine if you are asleep or awake while experiencing a vision. Often visions seem to unfold on a movie screen in your mind, and you simply observe without any control of your perception. There have been times that I felt I was "in between" being asleep and awake when these experiences occurred. I have awakened from a dream several times and was immediately caught up in a vision. Therefore, I had both simultaneously!

In Daniel 2:28, Daniel referred to Nebuchadnezzar as having both dreams and visions. In Daniel 7:1, it states that Daniel himself experienced a dream while visions passed through his mind. These passages confirm that they can occur simultaneously. It is important to note that Daniel was quick to document his experiences; he had visions and then "wrote" the dream, which is an example for us today to wake up and write: "In the first year of Belshazzar king of Babylon Daniel had a dream and visions of his head upon his bed: then he *wrote the dream*, and told the sum of the matters" (Daniel 7:1 KJV, emphasis added).

Many visions are referred to as "open visions." These can occur so quickly that perception of surroundings is completely lost. Open visions often appear to totally consume us. I have experienced open visions in which it seemed as though I was in a trance or even literally transported into another place or time. We can have what I refer to as "inward visions," a series of images that occur in your mind's eye. Also, an individual can have a revelation of God's purpose for his or her life, a personal vision of purpose and destiny—such as having a vision to be a pastor or for deliverance or other ministry. This is not the same as an open vision, a night vision or a dream; it is a heart-spoken call or direction.

Another Hebraic understanding of a vision is "to prophesy." This explains why dreams and visions are relevant to the prophetic ministry and the seer anointing. Many visions prophetically declare things that will come to pass in the future. The Hebrew word for "vision," *chazah*, also translates as a "divine communication," meaning also "to perceive or to see"; thus visions are meant to be a form of communication from the Lord.

I think we can safely say that visions are more of a visual perception of revelation that we see with our spiritual eyes. Unlike dreams, we can receive visions when our minds are awake and in the midst of daily activity, as well as during worship or prayer. They seem more real and literal than our dreams, which are more symbolic. Because visions are more "real," and are very often matter-of-fact (or clearer), they require little interpretation. For the most part, *what you see is what you get!* They should, however, be carefully considered and spiritually evaluated before sharing with others.

Once you understand that God desires to speak to you, you will become more sensitive to hearing and "seeing" His voice. Dreams and visions interplay in our lives in many different ways. A dreamer can have external visions, inward visions (in which you have a vision with your eyes closed or even open, with your spiritual eyes seeing a vision), visions within a vision, a dream in a vision or even a dream within a dream. Again, *nothing is always.* Definitions are not as important as the fact that God is speaking! Just as I promised to share my dreams with you, I will share visions also so that you can gain more understanding of how God speaks through both.

Different Ways God Communicates

God continues to establish generations that will hear His voice. In the Garden of Eden, God had intimate fellowship with Adam and Eve. Only when sin entered into the hearts of mankind did that communication become difficult. Since then, mankind has been distant from the Lord due to our sinful nature. But the

Lord's heart toward His people has not changed: He longs for companionship and communication with us, His chosen people. A close look at Hebrews 1:1–2 explains this:

> In the past God spoke to our forefathers through the prophets at many times and in various ways, but in these last days he has spoken to us by his Son, whom he appointed heir of all things, and through whom he made the universe.

Again, I have realized that God's people must not limit how God speaks to them. Dreams and visions are only two ways in which God communicates. He speaks both the *logos* (the written Word of God) and the *rhema* (an inspired word, either from the written Word or by one of the gifts of the Spirit). God has spoken to me in many different ways, and I am sure you have experienced the same. He speaks to me through the gift of discernment, having an inner "witness" in my spirit. He will speak to me through someone's preaching or teaching. He has even spoken to me through street signs, billboards and movies. Remember, God is a talking God!

Many times the Lord will speak through counselors and physicians. Physicians are often used by God to reveal certain physical situations that need prayer, and counselors can be of tremendous aid when we are dealing with crisis. God will use anyone who will be His vessel.

God has also spoken to me through nature. I have been inspired to write many sermons while in the mountains. I have also been inspired resting alongside a waterfall, meditating on the sound of water trickling over the rocks and pebbles. It would seem as if every sound were a whisper from God, a comforting experience of His everlasting love. The sound gave me a deeper connection with the Lord as I would meditate on Him.

Revelation 19:10 reads, "The testimony of Jesus is the spirit of prophecy"; in other words, when Jesus is present, prophecy is released. Prophecy simply means that God is speaking, whether to each of us personally or corporately. He will also speak through drama, prophetic gesture, demonstration, instruments, singing, books and many, many other ways. Have you ever heard a song that touched your heart, or read a book that gave you revelation? Well, precious one, God was speaking to you. There is more to Revelation 19:10 as it relates to the power of testimony: The word *testimony* basically means "Do it again, God!" Every time I write a testimony of what God spoke to me during a dream or vision, the Lord is, at that very moment, causing the words of that testimony to be sown into spiritual wombs so that He can do it again. A testimony prophesies that God wants to do the very same thing again. So, whenever you read my testimonies throughout this book, raise your hands and say, "God, do it again for me!"

God Is Always Speaking!

If we will be a people with open minds and open hearts, God will use many different methods to minister to us. Do not have a mindset about how God speaks. If we limit His ways of communication, we will not properly hear. Remember, it is His perfect will for us to know His voice!

Jesus said that His sheep hear His voice (John 10:27). The word translated "hear" in this passage is the Greek word *akouo*, which means "to be endowed with the faculty of hearing, not being deaf." In other words, it means that we have been endowed (I use my own word here: "fashioned") with the ability and purpose to hear God's voice and not be deaf to it.

Wow! Think about this: From the time of our creation, God purposefully placed within each one of His children the divine ability to hear His voice! He expects us to hear Him, and this proves He wants to talk to us. When I think about this, I visualize a Holy Ghost radio tower that is transmitting heaven's language, and placed within me is a receiver, like an antenna,

51

that directly tunes me in to hear His voice. This supernatural device gives me a direct line to my Father, and when He talks, I want to listen. This ability to hear His voice is confirmed in Numbers 12:6 (KJV): "And he said, Hear now my words: If there be a prophet among you, I the LORD will make myself known unto him in a vision, and will speak unto him in a dream."

Since the Fall of man, God has been speaking through prophets. Now He is training a prophetic people to communicate His will! Through sin, man has become dull of hearing, which is why the prophetic has been released: to address people in a way that they can hear God's voice again. People who are in tremendous sin are convinced that they are not worthy enough to hear from Him. Feeling condemnation, many falsely believe that He would not care to speak to them. This is the purpose for the prophetic movement and the release of God's voice—to encourage God's people with edification, exhortation and comfort. Those who desire to hear Him will be part of the prophetic generation. If you are a prophetic people (and you are!), then God wants to make Himself known to you in a vision and a dream.

I personally believe that because He "knew us" (implying intimacy) and "formed us" before we were in the womb, God placed His built-in receiver—the one that directly tunes us in to hear His voice—into our spirits before we were born. The enemy, however, had a plan to rob us of purpose and the ability to hear His voice. To be honest, we all have to have our receivers fine-tuned to His frequency in order to hear His voice. Dear one, many of us have not perfected that fine-tuning yet. Like tuning in a radio station, we have to find the correct frequency. Messages and signals come from other sources, like radio stations that we do not want to hear. This book is meant to help you do that: fine-tune your spirit to hear from God and empower you to discern the sources of the dreams and visions you receive.

Every receiver needs a transmitter. You are a receiver of dreams and visions, and when information comes to you in the night season, you have to determine what transmitter was used to bring you the dream. Let's call that the *source*. What are the sources from which we receive dreams? When we determine the source, we can determine the transmitter.

Is It Really God Talking?

Dreams come from several sources, but God is the primary source of dreams. He is *always* pursuing us—and gives dreams to both the saved and the unsaved!

Dreams and visions are as significant today as they were in biblical times. Remember, the Jewish culture always considered dreams and visions important—even if their hearts were hardened to the truths within the dreams. Jewish history proves that nothing in their lives is coincidental, especially not dreams. Know that God has never *not* spoken through dreams and visions—regardless of what your current mindset might be telling you.

The spiritual sources of true dreams and visions are always motivated by the Spirit of the Lord and communicated through our natural minds to relay a divine message. The message can be personal, but it can also be a message that relates to our families, the Church, our businesses, our nations and future events.

Another source of dreams is the natural man, which is where "soulish" dreams originate. Each of us is composed of body, soul and spirit. Our soul represents our mind, will and emotions. Since dreaming is a normal part of our physical bodies' function, many times our emotional condition is reflected through our dreams. What our minds are fixed on during the daytime will often appear in our dreams. We need to be cautious and not automatically assume that *every* dream is of divine origin. Rather, we carefully submit our hearts and minds to the Lord and patiently wait for the true interpretation. If the dream is from God, it is my belief that He intends to empower us with the interpretation—eventually! Again, remain patient while waiting to hear, and if He chooses never to answer with an interpretation, then ultimately He remains in control.

We must be careful not to confuse natural dreams with divinely given ones. And we must remain on alert when someone presents a dream to others as being from God. Scripture is very clear on this subject: "Thus saith Jehovah of hosts, Hearken not unto the words of the prophets that prophesy unto you: they teach you vanity; they speak a vision of their own heart, and not out of the mouth of Jehovah" (Jeremiah 23:16 ASV).

There is a healthy "need to know" within each of us—the level of certainty that each of us needs. We desire to be "certain" that what we hear or see is from the Lord. Being certain is part of our walk with the Lord; many times, however, certainty boils down to complete *trust*. What I am trying to convey is that many times we *cannot* be certain of an interpretation or that we have heard His voice properly. It is during these times that we must lock into complete trust. Hebrews 13:5 says that He will never leave us or forsake us, right? Therefore, it is *never* His plan that we be confused or uncertain of His love for us. This is one of the main reasons He gives us dreams and visions: It is a continual source of encouragement and empowerment.

The *unhealthy* need to know is linked strongly to the occult. How? Symbolism is full of revelation of heaven's hidden mysteries waiting to be discovered and received. Sometimes, though, it seems that God is silent. It is easy for us to get discouraged and open doors to occult activity when things just do not seem to click. Whether He is not speaking in dreams and visions for a season, or whether an interpretation lingers, there is a proper way to respond. There is a fine line between revelation and the occult.

The word *occult* means to "conceal; hide; keep secret and beyond human understanding." When we are anxious in understanding our dreams, we become controlling in our attitudes and motives (all connected to the occult), and, therefore, come closer to crossing the line. Notice the word *occult* refers to things "beyond human understanding." This means we can easily be led by a demonic spirit in interpretation as a result of our soulish desires to interpret dreams out of emotion, outside of God's timing or involving our personal wills in other ways.

Such demonic spirits are often called "familiar" spirits because they are familiar with the people they are attacking. They are connected to witchcraft, as we see in 1 Samuel 28:8, when King Saul asked a witch to communicate with a familiar spirit from the dead. In my life, I have seen demons set me up to fail by placing certain snares before me, fully expecting me to fall into sin. They knew me well enough to anticipate my reactions and to act accordingly.

False dreams and visions can be demonically inspired. Sometimes these types of dreams are even crafted by evil men. Such dreams originate within the realms of darkness and are many times "dark dreams." False revelation is given in dreams like this. We can look at Scripture to gain an understanding of false revelation, as in Acts 16:16–18, a biblical example of a slave girl who was motivated and controlled by both a spirit of divination and a python spirit (which I discuss further in chapter 5). This girl operated in witchcraft and fortune-telling; thus her revelation had a demonic origin—the occult realm.

Always remember that we must exercise spiritual discernment when receiving and interpreting dreams and visions. This is, however, nothing to fear! Dreams and visions from God have always released life to me. Sorting through them as to what source transmitted them is part of our training in discernment and our ability to "tune in" more to His guidance. Start tuning in *now*—listen to Him speak to you through dreams and visions!

3

God Changes Our Hearts through Dreams and Visions

*M*ickey, I can't feel my arms and legs!"

I sat up in bed with a pounding heart. Fear gripped me, and I had the feeling that I was at death's door. I shouted hysterically once again. "Mickey! I'm dying! I can't feel my arms and legs, and my heart is racing!"

My husband jolted from the bed. Fully alert, he reached over to comfort me. "What's wrong? What do you mean? Do you think you're having a heart attack?"

"Yes!" I said with certainty.

I was only 27 years of age, too young to experience heart problems, but I was not leading a "normal" adult life. I was 78 pounds, and the anorexia and bulimia that I had been suffering from for years were taking their toll on my body. The day of this crisis, I had swallowed a handful of diet pills. Yes, I had overdosed on drugs! Yet the pills were my only salvation in curbing the severe hunger pains that I tried desperately to ignore.

Though I knew what was *really* causing my heart to beat so rapidly, I would not divulge the truth about the diet pills. No one knew my secret. My family was aware of the drastic weight loss, but I lied that "nerves" and "excessive stress" were the culprits.

The bulimia was becoming such a problem that full days and sometimes weeks were spent eating and vomiting. Isolating myself from pain and reality was my only means of survival. The fear of being rejected by others was controlling my life, and I hid behind my skeletal frame, literally killing myself. I knew that if I told anyone about the diet pills, they would be taken away from me, so I kept my secret.

"Yes," I told Mickey, "I believe there is something wrong with my heart. I'd better go to the hospital."

Our daughter, Kim, was four years old. Awakened from all the commotion, she came into the room. "Daddy, what's wrong? Is something wrong with Mommy?"

"Yes, Kim. But she's going to be fine. I'm taking Mommy to the hospital to get some medicine," Mickey said as he dialed our family physician.

"No!" Kim whimpered. "No, don't take Mommy away!"

Mickey called the next-door neighbor next. "Something is wrong with Sandie. I think it's her heart. Can you come over and stay with Kim?"

Within minutes, we were in the car speeding to the emergency room. My heart was pounding even faster by now; I could barely catch my breath. Then what others say about seeing their lives flash before their eyes happened to me . . . I had an open vision.

I began to see pieces of my life, as though I were watching a movie. I was a toddler playing in the backyard of our home in Houston, Texas. Then my childhood years in Fort Worth, Texas, riding bicycles and playing with neighborhood friends. Then a vision of my husband, our years together and my unfulfilled vows. *Mickey,* I said under my breath as I watched, *I've lied to you. I've betrayed you with what I have done to myself.* Then I saw my daughter's face. How angelic she was as a baby. I was anorexic when I became pregnant with her; it was a miracle I was able to carry her to term. She was born a very healthy baby in spite of my physical weakness and starvation. As I gazed on her in the vision, I felt agony and pain like I had never known. My heart felt as if it were breaking because of an unfulfilled void. I was certain I was near death, and I began to beg God to allow me to live.

I have not been able to be a good mother to her, I told God. *Please let me live so I might take care of Kim.* I said these things silently, because I was completely unable to move my mouth. I was both crying and dying on the inside.

We drove to the emergency entrance. A nurse met us with a gurney, and I was quickly wheeled into a room. By now I was turning blue.

"Blood pressure cuff, heart enzyme test—get it all!" the nurse directed as she hurriedly pulled the drapes and left.

The next steps were the EKGs and other tests to determine the stability of my heart. The physician on call began to ask questions . . . uncomfortable ones, like "Are you taking any drugs?"

"No," I lied. "No drugs! I've never taken drugs." I bit my lip, hoping my secret would go unnoticed.

By now, I was certain I was dying. I began to pray again silently. *God, I don't want to die. Please save me and let me live. I'll do* anything *if You let me live!*

It seemed like hours before the doctor came into the room with his prognosis. "I can't find anything wrong," he said. "Her heart tests are normal; her blood work is good. . . . If it happens again, come back and we'll check you out again."

A deep sigh of relief came from within me. "Thank You, Lord!" I said. Silently I made a vow to God, a vow I would be unable to keep but meant to at the time. *God, I know I was dying. Thank You for letting me live. I will never take another diet pill, and I will begin eating first thing tomorrow.*

Changing Our Hearts

I have shared another very private portion of my life in hopes that you will understand that it was through a *vision* that the Lord brought healing from a life-threatening eating disorder. That vision is the first I remember having (besides demonic visitations I had as a child, which I discuss in chapter 12).

In that vision, God was revealing the condition of my heart—not my physical heart, my *spiritual heart*. Yes, He desired to change my heart—through a vision. I was a mess. I was a liar and a deceiver, I was dying, and the Lord was trying to get my attention so that He could change me. His desire was to deliver and heal me, and through a vision, for the first time, I heard the warning loud and clear—I would die if I did not change. The time was nearing when I would be forced to face the root problems that led to the anorexic behavior and emotional drug addictions. I needed to begin to work through my inadequacies and insecurities that were driving me toward an early grave. I desperately needed to develop a stronger relationship with God and understand His love for me. Eventually God brought me down that path (a story I will share in chapters 11 and 12). But it all started with a vision.

I believe that God's entire purpose for using dreams and visions is to continue to align our hearts, thoughts, lives and intentions with His eternal plan. I have heard it said, and it is very true, that dreams and visions are God's love language. I like to tell others what I wrote earlier: "He loves us so much that He is never *not* pursuing us!" Dear reader, He just never, ever stops passionately pursuing us. And, whether we care to admit this or not, it is really true: We do not know what is in our hearts! Only Gôd knows the true conditions of our hearts. And He will use dreams and visions to reveal what is in our hearts and guide us into truth. In Job 33:14–18 (emphasis mine), it is written,

> For God does speak—now one way, now another—though man may not perceive it. In a dream, in a vision of the night, when deep sleep falls on men as they slumber in their beds, he may speak in their ears and terrify them with warnings, to turn man from wrongdoing and *keep him from pride, to preserve his soul from the pit, his life from perishing by the sword.*

In this passage, it is clear that God will warn us in a dream or vision to protect us from wrongdoing, preserve our souls and keep us from pride. Haughtiness and pride must be addressed and repented of; yet many times we may not see it! In fact, many times we refuse to recognize our haughtiness, and God will speak to us concerning the issue through a dream or vision.

This is what happened to King Nebuchadnezzar. A very prideful and evil king, he had several dreams in which Daniel was used by God to interpret and minister truth to him. Daniel understood their purpose: "But as for me, this secret is not revealed to me for any wisdom that I have more than any living, but . . . *that thou mightest know the thoughts of thy heart*" (Daniel 2:30 KJV, emphasis added). The king's dreams would reveal the condition of his heart. Let's take a look at Nebuchadnezzar and his dreams as a guide for learning to recognize God's voice and directives in dreams and visions.

King Nebuchadnezzar's Heart Condition

Now, put down this book! Grab your Bible, and prayerfully and carefully spend quality time reading chapters 2–5 of the book of Daniel. In this passage you will read that God attempted to reveal the condition of the king's heart through a series of dreams. Nebuchadnezzar was an idol worshiper, and his heart was filled with pride. God relentlessly pursued Nebuchadnezzar through dreams, attempting to lead him into repentance. In fact, the entire biblical account of this king is laced with pride, arrogance and idolatry. All of these areas are serious heart conditions. Especially idolatry! All through Scripture we read that idolatry is a serious issue with God. God used Daniel as a mighty tool to help turn this king around, but it was not until Nebuchadnezzar completely lost his mind that he finally submitted to God!

Scripture does not actually say that the king "repented," but he did change. And the truth is that the word *repentance* means to "turn and change the way we think." Repentance is all about turning *from* our sin and *to* God. Dear ones, though we may have led lives of pride and arrogance, when God finally gets through to us, especially using a dream or vision, we need to run to God rather than away from Him! He is a God of forgiveness and grace.

The Lord faithfully pointed out the thoughts of the king's heart, even when he remained obstinate and haughty. The Lord was beckoning Nebuchadnezzar, through dreams, to see the pride rooted in his heart, repent and change. Instead, because he did not heed the warnings in his dreams, he grew *more* prideful. Nebuchadnezzar was on a slippery slope, headed for destruction, and God was attempting to get his attention. When he was at his lowest point, he finally lifted his eyes to heaven, and immediately his sanity returned! It was at that moment that God's grace gave him a helping hand out of that prideful pit, and the king honored the Lord. Finally, he had changed! He recognized that God was in complete control and that God was truly God! Even so, we do not read in Scripture that he actually repented, nor do we see a completely transformed life.

Repent and Turn

Believer, you are not reading this book by accident. Though you chose this book to read because you want to understand more concerning dreams and visions, you are also receiving powerful impartations of revelation concerning the condition of your own heart. I know I am hammering in King Nebuchadnezzar's journey, but it is very important to realize that God may be exposing pride and idolatry in our own lives by speaking to us in our dreams . . . just as He did with the king. Let me explain a bit more concerning issues of pride, as your future dreams may make reference to it. Pride in our own abilities is considered idolatry. Both were strongly rooted in my life, and I am writing with a desire that you be free of the pain I experienced—and I continue to tell my story with anticipation that you will be set free. I am all about freedom. Idolatry puts us in bondage and hinders our relationships with the Lord.

Idolatry is not limited to bowing down to an idol. It is much more than that . . . it is bowing down to any "false" image. This does not simply mean a carved wooden idol—it can be anything we believe about ourselves that is false, or anything false concerning God.

Think of it another way. What is your "image" of God? Do you have an image of Him as your healer, your provider and your deliverer? Or do you imagine Him to be harsh, judging and cruel? Dear ones, if our image of Him is *not* as the Word describes Him—and we believe the opposite of the truth concerning Him and His goodness—we are committing idolatry!

How is that? Because we are bowing down (giving reverence and respect) to a *false image*! If you have had a false image of Him, then simply repent (change your thinking). The enemy would love to use this type of unbelief against you by heaping condemnation on you. Simply say, "Lord, I'm sorry for bowing down to a false image concerning You." Then repent, turn away from that lifestyle and false belief system, and turn toward God and His Word once again!

In the same way, if we believe anything about ourselves that negates what God declares concerning us, we are committing a form of idolatry. Ouch! We cannot believe the lies of the enemy concerning God or ourselves!

I have written an entire book, *Silencing the Accuser: Eight Lies Satan Uses against Christians* (Chosen Books, 2011), on how the enemy attempts to falsely accuse us. I highly recommend reading it, as it will continually empower you and properly position you to receive, by faith, God's directives in dreams and visions. Precious saint, let's pay attention to our dreams—they will expose areas of our hearts that block us from walking in the fullness of life and heaven's blessings.

4

Dreams Reveal
Hidden Mysteries

*M*y intent through these early chapters is to lay strong foundations for more revelation. In the last chapter, you discovered one reason for God giving dreams and visions: to change our hearts. Before we explore more of these reasons, let me remind you that the Master Potter is at work, and He knows how to fashion us. He knows exactly what dream and/or vision we need . . . and when we need to receive it! As I said a bit earlier, He continues to mold you, fashion you and prepare you through your dreams and visions.

I use the word *fashion* on purpose. Why? Let's look at what the Amplified Bible has to say about renewing our minds with God's truths: "Do not be conformed to this world (this age), [*fashioned* after and adapted to its external, superficial customs], but be transformed (changed) by the [entire] renewal of your mind" (Romans 12:2 AMPC, emphasis added). It is important that we are continually fashioned and positioned spiritually to hear from the Lord. As we seek more revelation, we will be challenged to overcome mindsets, religious tradition and our human tendency to "reason." The things of God cannot be understood by our minds and intellects. They are heard and understood by the Spirit.

Sometimes God withholds revelation because if He gave insight into certain areas of our lives before we were ready, we would not be able to deal with it . . . nor understand it (see John 16:12). For us to fully receive God's truths, especially through dreams and visions, our minds must become fashioned by Him and renewed. With that in mind, know that as you continue to read, the Master Potter is at work, molding and fashioning you and your mind. You are being transformed. There is much to learn concerning your destiny and how God desires to bless you! If you have not done so yet, now is a great time to grab a pen or highlighter. Do not hesitate to write in the margins of this book or dog-ear the pages when the Holy Spirit reveals something to your heart. As you come to different times of self-reflection, you will want to refer back to those Holy Spirit–led markings!

Revealing Hidden Mysteries

Let's now look at another reason that God gives us dreams and visions, one that I love discussing: He desires to reveal hidden mysteries. God uses dreams and visions *to show what is in the heart of man and that He desires to reveal hidden mysteries to us.* These two are strongly connected: The condition of our hearts determines how easily and how often we will draw close to Him. Revelation is like a compass that challenges us to change our course and constantly head toward our true north. God deliberately conceals things so that we will draw near to Him to seek answers. As I have written repeatedly, dream language is about a lovingly relentless God who continually, obstinately and passionately pursues His people! The symbols and mysteries He uses to draw us nearer to His presence are a language of His love. Precious one, stay with me—you will thoroughly enjoy this read!

God's Mystical Language of Heaven

God purposefully speaks through dreams and visions using mystical symbols so that we will seek Him for the interpretations and prayerfully consider what He is revealing. It is almost impossible to interpret heaven's language without prayer. Many people attempt to interpret their dreams from a worldly view instead of God's way. This is dangerous! We cannot leave God out of the picture when interpreting our dreams; we *must* completely depend on the voice of the Holy Spirit for interpretation. God speaks in a heavenly language of symbolism. Spending time with Him opens the eyes of our hearts to interpret our dreams. Not hearing His voice concerning the meaning behind dreams and visions is like walking around in the dark without a light! God is the Light; therefore, we constantly need Him guiding our paths.

His main way of speaking in dreams and visions, in fact, is symbolism. Sometimes symbolism permeates a dream. Many people become simply overwhelmed at the thought of searching out the meaning, and they give up. Think about this, though: If God gave us only simple dreams and spoke directly, we would not search out the answers. Searching for answers requires hearing His voice and seeking revelation. If we did not have the mystery, we would miss out on opportunities to spend more time with Him! Mysteries within dreams demand that we go on a treasure hunt—how exciting is that?

There are times that I wished God would speak plainly in my dreams, but He simply does not work that way! There are, of course, exceptions, and He sometimes gives a very simple dream; but we cannot put God in a box. He will speak to us in ways He chooses. The main thing is that we are learning to hear His voice! Jesus said that His sheep hear His voice (John 10:4); therefore, we need to consider our dreams and visions as a training ground to hear Him more clearly.

Enlightening the Eyes of Our Hearts

We are commanded, as the apostle Paul did in Ephesians 1:18, to ask God to "open the eyes of our hearts" so that we see what He is revealing. In the amazing prayer of Paul captured in Ephesians 1, he writes about our hearts being enlightened (opened) to know our identities in Christ. I encourage you to take time to read the entire passage, in which he prayed that we fully understand our inheritance in Christ. This is powerful! Believer, we are sons and daughters of God (see Romans 8:14–15; 9:26; 2 Corinthians 6:18; Galatians 3:26; 4:5). We are not called "servants" but "friends" (see John 15:15 NKJV). This means that we have the privileges of sonship and friendship with the Lord, and we therefore have an inheritance provided for us because of what Christ accomplished at the cross.

It is the heart of God that each of us understands our identity—who we truly are in Christ. Unfortunately, many believers are in the midst of an "identity crisis." This is because they do not understand that they are already righteous in the eyes of God because of the finished work of Christ. Too many are still attempting to "prove" their worth through dead works. I know this firsthand because I was in an identity crisis for more than 35 years! I never felt worthy, acceptable or holy enough to please God. Therefore, I remained in a cycle of perfectionism, shame, fear and control for most of my life.

Thankfully, I began to have dreams that revealed the root of my identity issues, and I was set free from my past. You may be having similar dreams now that reveal strongholds of shame, inadequacy and lack of fulfillment. Dear one, this book is for you! *God wants us to come out of the wilderness of religious performance.* He is releasing dreams with heaven's language of deliverance. According to Matthew 15:21–28, deliverance is the children's bread. Therefore, God is feeding deliverance opportunities to you while you sleep! How awesome is that?

Most of us understand the idea of salvation. I was in a fundamentalist church for close to thirty years, and I knew that being "saved" meant I was "saved" from hell! To me, salvation was fire insurance. Since then, however, I have learned *all* that salvation provides for us. I want to explain this in detail, because what Jesus accomplished at the cross was much more than mere fire insurance!

The word we translate "salvation" comes from the Greek word *sozo*, which means not only being "saved" but also "delivered, empowered to prosper, protected and provided for"—I like to add, "Everything heaven has to offer!" When you received Jesus as your Savior, He provided *all* you need when He shed His blood at the cross as the sacrificial Lamb. (For those of you who want to further study the word *sozo* and all it means—all that occurred at the cross—I encourage you to read my recent book, *Power in the Blood: Claiming Your Spiritual Inheritance* [Chosen Books, 2013].)

Dear believer, keep a watch out for dreams that point to shame, disappointment, failure, inadequacy, lack of fulfillment, rejection and the like. God is speaking to those areas and revealing that *sozo* has already provided what you need. If you are having these types of dreams . . . get excited! This means that heaven's mysteries are being revealed to you so that you can be as free as God has promised.

Dreams Are Like Parables

I cannot impress upon you enough the importance of remembering that godly dreams are parabolic in nature. Like the parables of Jesus, the meanings of our dreams and visions are often "hidden" and "mysterious." This is why they are sometimes difficult to understand and interpret.

> As soon as He was alone, His followers, along with the twelve, began asking Him about the parables. And He was saying to them, "To you has been given the mystery of the kingdom of God, but those who are outside get everything in parables, so that while seeing, they may see and not perceive, and while hearing, they may hear and not understand, otherwise they might return and be forgiven." And He said to them, "Do you not understand this parable? How will you understand all the parables?"
>
> Mark 4:10–14 NASB

Did you notice that Jesus' disciples and followers asked for the meaning of the parables as soon as Jesus was "alone"? It is the same with us: Jesus wants to get alone with us, just as He desired to do with His disciples. He has special things to reveal and symbols to explain.

Jesus indicates that He speaks in parables so that those who truly seek Him will understand. He understood that those submerged in their modern-day religious system would not understand these parables because their hearts were hard and their religious mindsets would hinder their understanding. But God wants *everyone* to seek Him. Parabolic dreams are meant to cause us to hunger—and hunger drives us to seek the hidden mysteries. Yes, He desires to *reveal* what He has *concealed*!

Kings and Priests

A close study of Proverbs 25:2 (NASB) gives us a glimpse of what is in store for those who desire to hear His voice *and understand* it: "It is the glory of God to conceal a matter, but the glory of kings is to search out a matter."

Saint, it is your royal inheritance to understand heaven's language, for it is the glory of a king to search out a matter.

70

When you are given a dream and you go into search mode to understand it, it is counted unto you as a *glorious* thing! Proverbs 25:2 shows that it is God's divine nature, a glorious act, to "conceal" something in a dream or vision . . . but it is a glorious thing for you to become empowered to search out its meaning!

I can hear you saying, *I'm not a king . . . What does this have to do with me?* On the contrary—you *are* a king! Revelation 5:9–10 (NKJV, emphasis added) says this about our Lord:

> You are worthy to take the scroll, and to open its seals; for You were slain, and have redeemed us to God by Your blood out of every tribe and tongue and people and nation, and have made us *kings and priests* to our God; and we shall reign on the earth.

According to statistics, only 2 percent of Christians are priests; the rest are the "kings" that work outside the Church. The word *king* has several definitions—one who rules and has authority over a certain domain, for example. In the modern-day Church, however, marketplace ministers can consider themselves "kings" because they have a certain responsibility and authority in the domain of the workplace. Therefore, Proverbs 25:2 exhorts each of us, priests and kings, to search out the hidden meanings of our dreams and visions. In other words, it is our privilege!

> "For nothing is hidden, except to be revealed; nor has anything been secret, but that it would come to light. If anyone has ears to hear, let him hear." And He was saying to them, "Take care what you listen to. By your standard of measure it will be measured to you; and more will be given you besides. For whoever has, to him more shall be given; and whoever does not have, even what he has shall be taken away from him."
>
> Mark 4:22–25 NASB

God speaks mysteries and secrets that have hidden meanings . . . meant for those with a heart willing to search out the meaning. As we continue to "seek," we also develop ears to "hear."

Understanding dream language requires us to become "all ears"! Remaining attentive to God will become a lifelong skill, developed as we continue to seek Him.

Shifting into a New Season

God wants all of us to start well and finish well. I could write about many in the Bible who endeavored to do this, but because Jeremiah had a vision concerning starting and finishing well, I believe he is a good one to study. The first chapter of Jeremiah is very meaningful to me because it speaks of God's desire for us to start off right and then finish with power—and, by the way, this was revealed to Jeremiah in a vision!

God told Jeremiah that before he was even in his mother's womb, God *knew* him (see Jeremiah 1:5). The word for "knew" in this passage is the Hebrew word *yada*, and it means more than an intellectual knowledge of Jeremiah; it implies the intimacy of a husband and wife. We refer to this type of spiritual intimacy as "covenant." God knew Jeremiah's strengths, his weaknesses and the worst aspects of his self, and still He chose to remain in covenant. To me, this speaks volumes! And He does the same for us. He knows us before we are in our mothers' wombs, He knows our futures and He will do everything to continuously pursue us, empowering us to fulfill our destinies.

It is time for another short study on your own concerning God's empowerment through dreams and visions. I want you to shift into your new season, so take a few moments to read Jeremiah 1:5–12. Set this book aside and carefully read through this passage. Then answer the questions below:

1. How did Jeremiah see himself? (Describe the weakness he focused on concerning himself and his abilities.)

2. Describe how God saw Jeremiah. (What did God say that he was called to do?)

3. What did God do to Jeremiah's mouth?
4. What did Jeremiah see after this?
5. What did God promise to do (verse 12)?

Welcome back! I hope you took quality time to answer these questions. Now, let's discuss the vision of Jeremiah. This is important because God empowered Jeremiah to shift into a new season in order to fulfill his divine purpose. And He promises to do the same with us.

As you have been learning, God gives dreams and visions on *purpose*. In this particular vision, God encouraged Jeremiah and affirmed his calling as a prophet to the nations. In the vision, Jeremiah focused only on his weaknesses, protesting that he was too young and that he could not speak well. I believe that, in his heart, he doubted God's ability to change him and transform him to fulfill His divine purpose. God's answer was that He knew Jeremiah through a loving, covenantal relationship, and He had set him apart. I love that God also sets us apart. We each have a destiny, an assignment to fulfill. God gave Jeremiah a vision to affirm his anointing. Precious believer, God will give you dreams and visions to affirm your value to Him, also!

Then the Word says that God *touched* Jeremiah's mouth *with His hand* (verse 9) . . . and to me that is an awesome thought. The fact that the Potter's hand is once more involved in a vision is a powerful testimony of His love and mercy. But there is more! The Hebrew word *naga*, which is translated "touch," can also mean "to touch in a violent way." This was like a violent action or punishment against Jeremiah's enemy, and ours: doubt, unbelief and anything that hinders us from fulfilling our destinies. I believe that in this vision God violently judged Jeremiah's enemy—the accuser of the brethren—and empowered Jeremiah to fulfill his destiny.

The result of all this? Jeremiah was able to *see*. "What do you see?" God asked him (verse 11), and He was really asking, "*Now* what do you see?" Jeremiah saw the branch of an almond tree. Listen closely: The almond tree is the first tree that blossoms in a new season! You got it—Jeremiah saw his new season. He would no longer see himself as young, weak, disappointed and handicapped. God literally opened the eyes of Jeremiah's heart to see himself as God saw him! Even better, God told Jeremiah that He would watch over His word to Jeremiah to perform it (verse 12). Yes, Jeremiah's new season began with a vision that empowered him to fulfill his future.

Dear child of God, He is watching over every promise He has spoken to you. He may reveal your future in a vision, in a dream or even through His Word, but He wants you to start well (knowing you were intimate with Him at the beginning of time) and finish well (knowing He watches over His words concerning you). This is why it is so important to journal your dreams and visions . . . so you will not allow your disappointments to cause you to miss your next appointment with destiny. Symbolism in your dreams and visions will continue to reinforce that intimacy. Remember, it is a privilege to search out the hidden meanings. He wants to draw you near and speak hidden mysteries to you. He desires to share His world with you!

A Simple Activation for Visions

Now, take a few moments and worship Him. Worship prepares our hearts to hear the voice of the Lord—especially in dreams and visions. It is a way of activating your faith and your spirit to be able to hear. I often have visions while worshiping, and I believe that as you do this simple activation God will reveal something to you with a vision.

Put on some anointed worship music and spend time in His presence. As you sing and focus on the Lord, be open to the Holy Spirit to open your spiritual eyes and see into the supernatural. Keep in mind that you may have an "inward" vision with your eyes closed. It is still a type of vision, so do not negate it! Each time you worship, be prepared for Him to speak—whether in a vision or in another way. Every moment of worship is, after all, another opportunity to be activated for supernatural encounters. After your time of worship, write down any visions that you had—it is always important to document your dreams and visions—so that you will remember that *God* is talking to you!

W Want to hear God? Then worship!

O Offended at God because He seems silent? Then worship!

R Righteousness is a gift and not earned. Lost your identity? Then worship!

S Sons and daughters have a royal inheritance. Feel all is lost? Then worship!

H He loves us. Believing the lie that He does not care? Then worship!

I Intimacy is the by-product of pressing in. Cannot press? Then worship!

P Prepare for breakthroughs through your dreams. Think you cannot? Then worship!

5

Dreams That Influence Our Destiny

Destiny. It is a word tossed about in Christian circles—a lot! Most people believe that they are placed here on earth to fulfill a particular purpose. That is true, but—please hear me—there is much, much more to understand about our destiny. In fact, because everyone has dreams, I believe that God speaks to His children (believers and nonbelievers) in dreams that are designed to empower them to fulfill destiny. Before I get ahead of myself, though, let's define the word *destiny*.

The dictionary describes it as "events that will happen to a person or thing in the future." You will not find *destiny* in the Bible, and yet Scripture is laced with promises from God that are pregnant with destiny. Jeremiah 29:11, for example, says this: "'For I know the plans I have for you,' declares the LORD, 'plans to prosper you and not to harm you, plans to give you hope and a *future*'" (emphasis added). Destiny can be defined in this passage as plans that are intended to give us "hope and a future." The King James Version says it this way: "For I know the thoughts that I think toward you, saith the LORD, thoughts of peace, and not of evil, to give you an *expected end"* (emphasis mine).

Biblically speaking, then, destiny is "an expected end" and "God's plans for our future." We all have a destiny to fulfill. Each of us has goals that we desire to accomplish—and God has goals for us as well. God has a purpose for each of us, and we can be assured that whatever God promises us, He intends to fulfill it! My purpose in this book is to point out how much our dreams and visions affect our destinies. The potter envisions the finished product even as he or she begins to mold and shape the clay; when God uses dreams to mold and shape our lives, the end result is what He intended all along—His masterpiece, molded and fashioned into His own image. Each of us travels through our life journeys with missing pieces, and we need God's intervention to fill the void; He uses dreams and visions to complete each of us as a perfected vessel. Precious believer, He will visit us in the night season to impart dreams that empower us to fulfill our destiny.

This is why I like to use the term *destiny dreams*—God gives us dreams to empower us to be the best we can be, for ourselves and as sons and daughters to Him! As you continue to read, keep in mind that God knows where we are today. He will reveal hidden mysteries concerning our futures, but His heart is also to heal our todays with a plan to keep us moving toward complete fulfillment. All along, He is drawing us closer to Him, while at the same time healing and empowering us with hope, encouragement and divine fulfillment.

This is one reason that we need to pay close attention to our dreams, so that we can experience God's very best for our lives. Any dream can affect your destiny—depending on your properly responding to the message in the dream. I know I am hammering this in a bit, but it is extremely important to remember when documenting and interpreting dreams that the Holy Spirit is your guide!

In addition, we can benefit from the teaching of many people who have sought after the "glory of kings" in searching out the matter of God's dream language. I have been on a journey of studying dreams and visions for more than thirty years, and I have studied under numerous teachers. Literally thousands upon thousands of documented dreams have been examined, and most ministers, I believe, have come to the conclusion that dreams fall into common categories. In this chapter and the next, I will draw on much of what I have learned to help you understand your dreams by listing various dream types and suggesting things to note while documenting and interpreting them. This is not an all-inclusive list but a summary of the destiny-type dreams that I personally find to be the most common. (These are not listed in order of importance.) Though my suggestions do not provide *everything* you need to empower you to interpret your dreams, they will, I hope, serve as a guide as you grow in your understanding of your world of dreams.

Dreams from the Holy Spirit

Destiny dreams and dreams about our future are often prophetic in nature. Whenever the Lord ministers to us about possessing our personal Promised Land, we realize that we, like Israel, have to drive out the previous tenants who had settled in the land. Each of us has promises from God to possess. Certainly, many of those promises have already been accessed in life, but what about those that have not? It is the areas in our lives that still need perfecting, encouraging and fulfilling that God cares about. Dear one, He is all about you being prosperous and successful, having a hope and a future, just as Jeremiah wrote.

Dreams from the Holy Spirit will always impart hope and life. Remember, though, that He cares so much for us that He will also instruct and correct us so that we do not waver or fail. A fundamental principle for operating in dream interpretation is to always remember who the Holy Spirit is (His character) and how He operates in the realm of the prophetic on the earth. The Holy Spirit's character is described by many names and titles that describe His ministry: Comforter, Counselor, Advocate, Convicter of Sin, Intercessor, Revealer, Spirit of Truth and Teacher. Yet another description is *Breath*. Thus our dreams from the Holy Spirit are meant to give breath or life to us. Never does the Holy Spirit bring condemnation to a believer. Though our sins may be pointed out, it is always with an extension of grace and a helping hand to lift us up and out of the miry clay.

Dreams from the Holy Spirit reveal God's ultimate plan for our lives (even though interpretations may take a while!). They counsel us along the way, they speak truth into hidden places that have concealed lies, and they lead us along paths of righteousness. In 1 Corinthians 14:3 we read that the spirit of prophecy is meant for edification, exhortation and comfort. This, then, will be our plumb line for interpreting dreams from the Holy Spirit.

Dreams of Edification

The word translated "edification" means, in Greek, "to build up." I would label a dream an "edification dream" if it made you feel great about your life. You awake feeling on top of the world, that you have risen above present challenges. Interestingly, the Greek word for *edification* is related to the word that means "rooftop." How many times have you felt "on top of the world"? Edification dreams bring about this response.

As I mentioned, 1 Corinthians 14:3 ties the prophetic ministry to edification, exhortation and comfort. Therefore, when God speaks through dreams and visions, His heart is to do exactly that—*not to condemn*. Even dreams of correction are always meant to bring hope. If you are in a dry season, experiencing despair and depression, you will awake from an edifying dream with hope and renewed encouragement. Even if you do not remember the details of the dream, you will still awake completely refreshed when God gives you a dream of edification. How does this happen? Remember that your dreams and visions bring not only revelation but also an impartation. Isn't that exciting? An edifying dream imparts edification to your spirit.

Dream of Lockhart, Texas. Twenty-five years ago, when I was a young pastor, I went through a rough time when I doubted my ability to hear God. This caused me to withdraw from fully embracing my position as a spiritual leader. In fact, I reasoned with the Lord that I was not called or anointed enough. One night in a dream, I heard the Lord say, *Lock your heart back into Me during the month of June.* Two months later (during the month of June), while traveling to south Texas, I started complaining to God again. When we had to stop for gas, I noticed a road sign that said, "Welcome to Lockhart, Texas." Suddenly, my cell phone rang. It was my administrator, who wanted to tell me about *her* dream.

"Pastor, the Lord spoke to me in a dream! We are supposed to lock our hearts into God during this month—the month of June."

I was stunned . . . yet amazed. I looked again at the road sign. We were definitely in Lockhart, and it was definitely the month of June. It shifted me into faith. I locked my heart back into the Lord and His purpose for my life. I immediately put my "pastor's hat" back on and surrendered to my destiny in ministry.

Dreams of Exhortation

Exhorting dreams and visions give a message of encouragement. The dream often serves as a call to become motivated to action. I like to refer to these types of dreams as "courage" dreams; while edification dreams produce a sense of hope, exhorting dreams purposefully produce greater levels of faith.

Similar to edifying dreams, upon awakening from these types of dreams, you have a renewed motivation to get busy doing the work of the Lord.

I have had many dreams that involve spiritual warfare. In the dreams, demonic forces have actually named themselves. I was not fearful during the dreams, nor did I awake fearful. Rather I awoke knowing the assignment of the enemy, and I felt equipped and exhorted to move forward with spiritual warfare and take authority over all demonic functions. Courage had been imparted to me in the dreams; therefore, I was empowered to strongly engage in the battle with courage and faith.

Dreams of Comfort

Comfort dreams are designed by the Lord to heal us—body, soul and spirit. Many times we carry past pain and painful memories with us, while the Lord's desire is for us to be completely healed from emotional pain, trauma and anything that might hinder us from experiencing life to the fullest. A comfort dream is not designed to empower someone to remain in his or her comfort zone. I have realized that when I am comfortable, I am settling for much less than God has for me to achieve and do in Him. Rather than letting us remain "comfortable" with past fears and weaknesses, a comfort dream challenges us to believe that God will heal us from the past, comfort us during difficult and dry seasons and minister His love to us whenever we feel at a loss.

My comfort dream. In a powerful dream of comfort, I was lying on my back in soft, white sand. Next to me was a most beautiful waterfall. I basked in the warm sunlight, enjoying the peaceful sound of the water flowing over the falls. Suddenly, Jesus was sitting beside me. He placed His hand on my stomach (I knew in the dream He was touching my innermost being) and said, *I have come to give you comfort and . . .*

While Jesus was still speaking, I woke up! Right away I realized that I did not know what else Jesus said He had come to give me. I was actually angry at myself because I could not remember. As I pressed my memory for the details of my dream, I recalled that the word I could not remember started with the letter *c*. So I pulled out a dictionary, just to realize how many awesome words begin with the letter *c*—courage, credibility, certainty, clarity, care, celebration, change, chosen and on and on and on!

I finally understood that Christ had come to give me much more than just comfort. He deliberately caused me not to remember the last word because He wanted me to pray and search out the full meaning of the dream. Believe me, I needed all the other words I found that began with a *c*!

Dreams with Recurring Themes

Recurring dreams are a strong indicator that God wants us to bring forth something new or cause us to change. If we are ignoring the dream and not responding properly by embracing the change, it might be repeated. Once new behavior occurs, the dream will probably cease.

Dreams of Teachers, Tests and Schools

Dreams of being in school have been among the most common for me. It seems as if I am always *learning* something! Maybe it has been because I have made so many mistakes (and, in my life, have I ever!). On a good note, however, a dream about school could mean that I am remaining teachable and that my future involves growing and being perfected in Christ. We are always being perfected in God and being tested for promotion, right? I continually praise God for His faithfulness to teach me the error of my ways and deliver me from darkness. I bet you can relate to dreams about going to school, also. Let's take a look at how to interpret them.

In these types of dreams, the dreamer may be learning something new. Maybe the dreamer is in the midst of a "learning curve." The dream could represent a current process of taking different types of tests or be an indication that something was not learned the first time around. Tests are often needed for a promotion.

I have had many dreams in which I am in college and I am searching for my next class. This was an indication that I needed guidance—or perhaps that I had graduated and should not feel that I still needed to remain a student! Spiritual maturity may be the answer to remaining in an old pattern of training. Things to consider:

- Note the people present. Was there a teacher, a principal, another classmate or classmates? If you were in the principal's office, it may mean that God has something specific to talk to you about.
- Were you in high school? This could represent the Holy Spirit (HS) School, and the Spirit is training you or desires to elevate your gifting.
- Are you retaking the same test? This could mean it is time to cycle out of your wilderness (pass the testing phase!) and move forward.

Dreams of Vehicles

Most of the time, dreams of vehicles symbolize someone's calling, ministry, vocation or purpose in life. Vehicles represent what you are called to do. I have had many dreams in which my vehicle also represented the anointing. Keep in mind that vehicles move you from one point to another; therefore, dreams with vehicles could represent the fact that you are moving forward into another season or point of entry.

- Make note of the type of vehicle. Larger vehicles—a bus, plane or cruise liner—often symbolize larger callings, ministry and influence. A car or a small boat or plane could symbolize an individual calling or smaller ministry.

- Make note of the color, size, style and/or type of vehicle. Think outside the box—unicycles, tricycles, horses, mules and camels are vehicles also.

- Note who is driving. Is it you? Is it someone you know? Does the person have no face or name? Is it someone from your past? Someone from your past could mean that an old emotion or relationship is driving you. Emotions play a huge role in interpreting this type of dream. A past relationship could be "driving you crazy" with negative emotions or influencing your future in a negative way. Most of the time when no face is revealed for the driver, it is the Holy Spirit. This is awesome, for it shows you that the Holy Spirit is directing (driving) your life!

In many of my dreams, I am in my car, and for years I was the one driving. This was an indication that I wanted to be in control. Being a prophetic "seer," I believed that these dreams indicated that I was the visionary in the ministry. To some degree this was true; because of my control issues, however, I believe now that the Lord was ministering to me about that stronghold. After I was delivered, there came a dream in which I was in the backseat of my car. The driver had no face—a symbol that the Holy Spirit was driving! God had been faithful to move me from one point to the other.

Dreams of Storms

Storm dreams are also very common. They have often been interpreted as negative dreams. Remember, nothing is always!

Storms can clear the air and move obstacles out of the way that are not sturdy. Sometimes these dreams are hinting that something is on the horizon. They often encourage us that the future is being unveiled! Here are some other thoughts to consider:

- Storms often result in emotions of fear to the dreamer. If there is fear throughout the dream, it is quite possibly a dream of warning.
- Note the color of the storm. Light and bright colors might mean that God is bringing something positive your way. If they are dark or muted, however, the dream might refer to a destructive force headed in your direction.
- Many times, storm dreams are meant for intercession and spiritual warfare prayer. Those with a keen discerning of spirits have these types of dreams often. Though intercession and spiritual warfare target demonic attacks, these dreams can also represent showers of God's blessings and are to be prayed through and enjoyed! As with dreams of vehicles, emotions will help determine the direction of your prayers.

Dreams of Clocks and Watches

Dreams with timepieces often reveal a particular season or time in the dreamer's life. Since many clocks have an alarm, the dream may be a form of "wake-up" call. It often comes as a warning to the dreamer himself/herself. It is possible that we need to wake up to the wiles of the enemy. Satan does not want you to fulfill your destiny!

Sometimes these types of dreams are meant to be an intercessory burden for a nation. This happened to me in South Korea in 2014; I had a wake-up call in the form of a dream/vision. I awoke and experienced an angelic visitation from an "awakening angel" who was sent with a message to the Body of Christ to wake up to their purposes in God.

- Is there a specific time shown during the dream? If it is 11:00, it might symbolize that you are in transition (the number eleven). If the hands on the clock or watch point to 6:00, it might symbolize works of the flesh that the Lord wants to deliver you from. (Numbers carry various meanings in Scripture, and I have listed these meanings in chapter 9.)
- God told Jeremiah He would "watch" over His promises to Him (see Jeremiah 1:12). A dream of a watch might mean that God is reminding you of the same promise!

Dreams of Flying or Soaring

Flying dreams are very common destiny dreams. In a strongly encouraging way, they most often represent an ability to rise above problems and move in the spirit realm. These dreams are highly inspirational and often an encouragement from God to press into the supernatural and revelatory realm.

- Soaring dreams are most always inspirational and are not demonic in nature. Common emotions are exhilaration and feeling closer to God.
- Whenever we are *ascending* in a dream, we usually awake being inspired and empowered. This type of dream can be an encouraging dream to remind us of our true identity in Christ. According to Scripture, we are seated with Christ in heavenly places and are above all principalities and powers (see Ephesians 2:6). Remember, also, that the Word says in Mark 9:23 that nothing is impossible for us who believe. Therefore, this type of dream makes us feel that we are "above" all challenges.

Dreams of Nakedness

Dreams of nakedness often point to our need to become more vulnerable and intimate with God and others. On the other hand, they could mean that we feel exposed and too vulnerable. When interpreting these types of dreams, one has to discern the context. Emotions are also very important to document. If during the dream you feel fear and shame, it might be considered a type of exposure, or even vulnerability to past memories, which often stir up shame and guilt. In some cases, especially if the dreamer is in the midst of great spiritual warfare, it can symbolize that the dreamer is not fully dressed in his or her spiritual armor, and it emphasizes the need to put it on. These types of dreams occur very often when the dreamer is in transition. Fear of a new challenge, a new job or spiritual promotion might stir up feelings of inadequacy and a belief that "I am not properly equipped"—hence, naked.

In the past, before I experienced deliverance from generational strongholds, I had many dreams in which I was naked. I would awake from those dreams feeling unclean and exposed. Though I was seeking deliverance from many different strongholds, I was ashamed of my past. I was a "closet person" who attempted to keep everything hidden. And when I came out of that closet, so to speak, and began to confess my problems, the shame grew even worse. I had these "naked" dreams until the day I experienced deliverance. After the Lord set me free, I never had one again. Hallelujah!

- Make special note of the setting. Are you before a large crowd? Are you publicly speaking? If so, you may have a fear of being "exposed" as an unqualified speaker. Surveys indicate that fear of public speaking is the number one fear! If you are fearful in your dream, the Holy Spirit may be speaking to you concerning your identity in Christ.

- Are you in a phase of transition? Transition often brings fear. The Lord may be encouraging you to trust Him more as you fulfill your calling.

Dreams of Being Unprepared

I have had several recurring dreams in which I went to preach in a church but had left my message and Bible at home. Each time I awoke, I felt gloomy and fearful. The interpretation is that I feel unprepared whenever I minister, and I have an underlying fear that I will not make a good impression. This fear goes way back into my childhood, for I often dealt with insecurity. I have learned to trust the Holy Spirit when I minister; this type of dream, however, seems to arise when I am battling intimidation. Many times the dream has been from the Lord—revealing a fear that I need prayer for and deliverance from. At times, though, I have been certain that the dreams were demonically inspired. Remember, the devil loves to intimidate God's children because it keeps us from stepping out with boldness and confidence as we teach or demonstrate the Word.

- Also make note of the setting in these types of dreams. Are you at your place of employment? Your church? Does it take place in a family setting? Carefully examine your life and determine if you deal with fear of failure. If so, does it occur while you are filling a certain role in a particular place? Your dream may be revealing a deep and emotional fear of not measuring up or feeling intimidated.
- Find specific Scriptures that speak to you positively concerning your identity in Christ. Also, think about your self-talk. Our minds are always chattering away, and if we are going to be saying something, it needs to remain positive. If you are thinking negatively about yourself too much, it may be showing up in your dreams!

89

Dreams about Teeth

I have realized that most of the time dreams concerning teeth reveal the need for wisdom. In the dream, pay attention to the wisdom tooth—is it missing, decayed or broken off? If so, wisdom may be needed. These dreams are often connected with the dreamer's ability to make wise decisions or the ability to understand a situation. Remembering that nothing is always, I often think of Solomon and how he asked for wisdom, and, because of that, prosperity was his reward. Many times when needing a financial breakthrough, people have dreams about their teeth. I have often counseled businesspeople to "seek *first* the kingdom" (and kingdom wisdom) . . . and all other things (finances) will be added.

When I was a teenager, I wore braces. I had the most crooked front teeth you have ever seen. I was always embarrassed whenever I smiled. So I was thrilled to get braces! Later in my life, when I was pastoring a local church, I had continual dreams about those two front teeth with braces. I prayed for the interpretation for what seemed like days. I was aware that teeth in a dream often referred to needing wisdom, but, though I understood the wisdom connection, I could not make the dream come together.

I fretted over this very simple dream. It should have been easy to interpret: I need wisdom. Plain and simple, right? And yet I could not get peace about my interpretation. Months later I got it in full: I was to "brace" myself because of a coming situation, and if wisdom was not applied to the equation, there would be a tendency for me to feel ashamed. I am exceedingly thankful that the Holy Spirit spoke this to me; it happened just as this simple dream warned me.

- If teeth appear to be falling out, then it is highly possible that God is communicating the need or inability to properly discern and understand a situation.

- Note which tooth is the main focus. The wisdom tooth deals with wisdom, and the eye (seer) tooth deals with revelation. False teeth represent false teaching or false wisdom received.

Dreams of an Ex or Past Relationships

Dreams of any type of ex—boyfriend, girlfriend, wife, husband, employer, friend, etc.—are common warnings from God about returning to past behavior or old belief systems. Dreaming about past relationships does not literally mean that an old "flame" or relationship is being rekindled or revisited. Most of our dreams are intrinsic, meaning God is dealing with us directly in motive, heart issues, pain, trauma, etc. An old relationship could be symbolic of an old habit, and God is warning us to *not* make ungodly covenant with it again! On the other hand, in a positive sense, God might be restoring a relationship that has appeared lost.

As senior pastor of a local church, I have often had dreams about those who have left our fellowship. Pastoring is difficult at times because our hearts become connected to those for whom we care. Whenever I dream these types of dreams, I go to the Lord in prayer and ask Him if there is any unforgiveness to be dealt with concerning the relationship. I also seek His directives concerning the people in my dreams—should I guard my heart in a new relationship that is coming into my life and/or be careful as the relationship develops? It is of utmost importance to depend on the Holy Spirit to guide you in interpreting these types of dreams.

- Note who the person is and what he or she represents to you. Dreaming about an ex may mean that you are having regrets, but it does not necessarily mean you should reengage in the relationship.

- Most likely the Lord is attempting to uncover a certain incident that needs healing in your heart. Examine the relationship carefully; what was positive, what was negative? The Lord will lead you in how to pray.

Dreams of Dead Relatives

Dreams of people who have passed away, especially if the dreams concern parents and/or grandparents, can indicate generational issues that are at work within the dreamer's life (blessings and curses). The gift of discernment will be required to receive the blessings or cut off the curses. Paying close attention to emotions during these dreams will prove beneficial when interpreting.

Because I have needed so much deliverance due to generational strongholds of shame, fear and control, I have dreamed numerous times about generations in my family—both good things I have inherited through the bloodlines as well as bad things I have inherited. Because I have Creek Indian heritage, I have documented hundreds of dreams revealing generational curses connected to my Native American lineage that had to be broken off of my life. I am eternally thankful to a loving Father who never stopped pursuing me! I am the "freed one" today because of dreams and visions . . . and the cross.

- Being fearful in the dream is a key sign of a generational stronghold of fear. This can be true of other emotions such as shame, terror, trauma, pride and so on.
- A poverty mentality is often prevalent in dreams. Dreams of an old farmhouse with no plumbing, electricity or heat that earlier generations once possessed is a clue that you have a generational curse of poverty that needs to be broken off your life . . . and the lives of future generations.

- Again, nothing is always! For years I complained about my Creek Indian heritage. One day my mother said to me, "Sandie, have you ever thought about the good things passed down through your generations?" Her words stopped me in my tracks—I think I even gasped for breath! She continued, "The Creek Indians were notorious for their courage and bravery. Maybe you should thank the Lord that you have a generational blessing to rely on when needed. You are a woman of great courage, and it probably came from that heritage!" Her eyes pierced right through me as she shook her index finger in my face. It was true, and I needed to hear it . . . from my mom of great wisdom!

Identity Dreams

Identity theft is real! We know about it in everyday life, but during the night seasons the Lord will reveal how the enemy of our souls has attempted to steal our *spiritual* identities. These types of dreams will usually feature our homes, families, livelihoods, ministries, relationships with God and more. Additionally, these dreams may take place in the past, present and/or future.

According to the dictionary, the word *identity* refers to "the quality of beliefs or conditions that make a person or a group different from others." It is amazing to me that most of us spend most of our lives attempting to fit in and *not* be different . . . yet God has deliberately made each of us different and unique!

My background is rooted in much fear of rejection, and once I was falsely accused by someone who was close to my heart. I prayed to the Lord, asking why people close to me seem to betray me as often as they do. As a result, the Lord answered me with a dream about my wallet being stolen.

It was a very simple dream that needed little interpretation. We carry all sorts of identification in a wallet—personal ID, driver's license, student ID and so on. The dream meant the enemy was attacking my identity and challenging all that I am in and through Christ Jesus (my spiritual authority, spiritual inheritance, identity as a daughter of God, etc.). Dreams of losing a purse or wallet are very common identity dreams. Most of the time, God is communicating that the dreamer has lost or is looking for his or her purpose, identity and favor. As I was when I dreamed of losing my wallet, most likely the dreamer is in an identity crisis.

Many people have been misled to think that these dreams are about finances . . . either the lack of them or an expectation of financial breakthrough. Once again, nothing is always. When I have had dreams of this nature, they have most often been about my identity. For years I suffered because I did not know my identity in Christ, and I believe that many others have suffered from many of the struggles that I have had to overcome. If God gives you a dream of this nature, the first place to look is within yourself; examine your identity. A lifestyle of rejection, abandonment, pressure to measure up, need to prove oneself through works—all of these are signs that you are in an identity crisis.

It has been my personal experience that many (many!) dreams fit in the category of identity dreams, because the devil does not want us to know who we really are! If we really knew who we were in Christ, the devil would not be as active in our lives (businesses, governments, churches, etc.) as he is. I am working continually on this . . . I know you are, too. Get ready, for God is going to download into you much about your identity in Him. As He does, you will rise up and exercise your spiritual authority over the powers of darkness that have attempted to hinder you from living your life in victory.

Dreams That Reveal Our Hearts

I discussed God's intent to reveal the conditions of our hearts through dreams in chapter 3. Because King Nebuchadnezzar's dream in Daniel 2 was also a destiny-type dream, however, it deserves more time for study and godly introspection.

Dear believer, listen up! We do not know our own hearts. I know, we think we do—but we do not. To fulfill our destinies requires that we continually allow the Lord to tender our hearts. Let's look at what God says about the lack of our own ability to discern the condition of our hearts:

> The heart is more *deceitful* than all else and is *desperately sick*; Who can understand it? I, the LORD, *search the heart*, I test the mind, even to give to each man according to his ways, according to the results of his deeds.
>
> Jeremiah 17:9–10 NASB, emphasis added

Notice that God "searches" the heart. This is the Hebrew word *chaqar*, which is translated "to search (out)" and "to seek (out)"; but interestingly it is a primitive root that means "to penetrate and examine intimately." This tells me that when God is searching out the conditions of our hearts in His very intimate way, His intention is to penetrate us deeply with His divine love and bring forth transformation. If we look once more at King Nebuchadnezzar's heart condition, we can completely understand how God desires to give dreams and visions to reveal the conditions of our hearts.

Dream of the blue car and black scarf. I was born from generations of pride, envy, control and competition. Over the years, when God was delivering me from destructive patterns, I had many dreams concerning those generations. In one of them I was driving a blue car; in fact, it was the car that I actually drove at the time. I was on a twisted, curving road, trying very hard to maintain control of the car. Then my car died. I got out and noticed that I had a very long, black scarf around my neck. It was so long that it dragged on the ground. Dream over.

It took me years to understand this dream because I did not understand God's dream language. Later in life, when I began to go through deliverance, I kept remembering this dream. Whenever we dream of a car, it usually represents our anointing or calling. Notice that I was doing the driving? This meant I was in control, and was I ever a control freak—in every way! The road was twisting and turning, meaning my path was not straight but crooked. The car died in the dream, which represented the death of the old nature. The sin nature of Sandie Freed was going to have to die so that I could put on the new man. The long, black scarf represented a long line of generational strongholds (demonic strongholds represented by the black color) that were negatively affecting me.

When I went through deliverance, I recalled this dream, and we broke off generational patterns of control, jealousy, envy, strife and more. It is clear now that, while God was giving me dreams that revealed the condition of my heart, this dream was also meant to lead me to later deliverance, which I very much needed.

Dreams of Deliverance

Dreams of deliverance are very common. In fact, as I have mentioned, the Word says that deliverance is the children's bread! (Mark 7:29–30 describes the deliverance of the Gentile woman's child.) For years, however, these types of dreams have gone unnoticed because too many believers do not recognize their need for deliverance, or they believe they are unworthy to receive it. Because of their importance, and because they involve my personal testimony, I have devoted two entire chapters to the subjects of deliverance and generational strongholds (chapters 11 and 12). This is mainly because God used dreams to save my life, and I was saved through the prophetic Word of the Lord and deliverance.

God is our deliverer! Exodus 3:8 describes His heart to deliver His children from bondage. One of my favorite passages of Scripture is Psalm 18:2, which describes God as not only our rock (our stability) and fortress (tower of protection and strength) but also our deliverer: "The Lord is my Rock, my Fortress, and my Deliverer; my God, my keen and firm Strength in Whom I will trust and take refuge, my Shield, and the Horn of my salvation, my High Tower" (AMPC).

The Hebrew word for "deliverer," *palat*, implies that He wants us to be safe, and also that He wants us to slip out of the clutches of the enemy! The word *anointing* means "to smear with oil." I like to tell people that the anointing (oil) on their lives will cause them to slip right out from the yokes of the enemy. If the devil tries to grab them, they will slide out of his grip into a greater outpouring of the anointing. In *The Jezebel Yoke: Breaking Free from Bondage and Deception* (Chosen Books, 2012), I write about how to break free from the enemy's yokes. Though I target mainly the Jezebel spirit, you will find this book helpful as you "slip" out from under the oppression of the enemy!

Dreams about Bathrooms

Many times deliverance dreams are revealed through "cleansing dreams" involving flushing toilets and bathrooms. David described the person who was able to ascend to the mountain of the Lord and stand in His holy place: someone with clean hands and a pure heart (see Psalm 24:4). As a destiny dream, dreams of bathrooms (including toilets, showers and baths) indicate that God is cleansing an area of the dreamer's life in order to empower the dreamer to ascend in his or her relationship with Him. It is also symbolic of God "flushing" something away from the dreamer's life that might impact the dreamer's future. There are plenty of people who feel that bathroom dreams are shameful, but they are not! Remember, deliverance is the children's bread, and many times bathroom dreams represent deliverance. This is because deliverance has a cleansing effect.

One year, while my husband and I were pastoring Faith Christian Center in Bedford, Texas (we are currently pastoring Lifegate Church International in Hurst, Texas), I felt very strongly that the Lord wanted me to begin teaching a series on how to host the presence of the Holy Spirit. As I taught, I emphasized the need to freely express ourselves in worship. Whether it be with lifted hands, closed eyes, dancing or kneeling, we needed to be free and unconcerned about what others thought of us. Each time I released the congregation, most of the people would just sit there . . . as if in some type of stupor. It grew worse as I taught, almost to the point that I could not even get many of them to lift their hands! I became so troubled about this that I would end each prayer at night with *God, please do something!*

Dream of flushing toilets. God answered with a very simple dream. In the dream, all of the toilets in the church began to flush . . . over and over and over, all at once. I awoke after several flushes and was wide awake.

I knew that God was speaking to me about a spiritual cleansing and deliverance. The next time I taught, I led the congregation in a prayer of repentance concerning pride issues and the fear of making a mistake. At the end of the prayer, I had the worship leader lead us in worship, and God's presence immediately manifested. People were crying, rejoicing, dancing, shouting . . . it was truly a deliverance! If it had not been for the directional dream revealing that corporate deliverance was necessary, we would not have experienced such a remarkable and glorious breakthrough. How glad I am that He is faithful!

Dreams of Direction and Instruction

Directive dreams can be extremely prophetic. Many times, directive and instructive dreams provide solutions when we are being challenged in fulfilling our destiny. I have had people tell me that the Lord instructed them in a dream as to which medications to take when they were ill. Sometimes direction was given as to what a person's vocation should be. Through dreams I have been given divine instruction as to how to properly lead our church congregation while teaching on certain subjects. I even had a dream that gave me direction for outlining and writing one of my previous books.

At times, these dreams give direction for prophetically praying into the dream and seeing it fulfilled. For instance, my dream of the blue car and the black scarf directed me toward the need for deliverance, with instructions that involved breaking off generational curses. In directive dreams, however, there is more of a sense of urgency.

Some examples of very clear directive dreams are found in Matthew 2, in which God warned the wise men not to return to Herod after visiting the infant Jesus (see verse 12). Clear dreams were also given to Joseph, the earthly father of Jesus, to take various routes for their protection (verses 13, 20, 22).

Many times God has given me dreams of direction and instruction when I have ministered in a different city, state or nation. It is not uncommon for me to have dreams like this when I travel. Sometimes they are for intercession and prayer, and other times the Lord uses the dream to insert direction into the ministry time. These directive words usually come packaged with a desire for a greater dimension of God's presence and glory. Directive dreams help us see further down the road than we presently are and help us avoid many pitfalls along the way of fulfilling divine destiny.

Dreams of Going through Doors/Opening of Gates

One type of directional dream is a dream of doors or gates opening. In most situations, these indicate that a change is coming. It has been my experience that when I have these dreams, I am either experiencing new opportunities or they are becoming available soon. When we dream of a closed door that begins to open, it can mean that advancement and promotions are opening up to us—new opportunities and new ways. New advancements are just beyond a closed door. Doors have a threshold, and when we move past the threshold, we enter a place of enlargement.

On the negative side, however, at every threshold we face the possibility of encountering something called a "python spirit" against which we must contend as we enter into increase. A python spirit is a spirit of divination and witchcraft; the Greek word translated "divination" in Acts 16:16, for example, is actually *python*. In English, a python is a large, muscular snake that kills its prey by constricting it until the prey suffocates, and this is a good picture of how the python spirit operates.

When a child is birthed, a "squeeze" pushes the baby into the birth canal, a very narrow place; once through, the baby crosses a threshold—an entrance—and is birthed into the world. The python spirit distorts this process by attempting to squeeze the life out of us any time we cross over, enter into a place of enlargement or pass over a threshold. At the place of breakthrough, it tries to wring the breath out of us in order to abort our divine destiny. As I pointed out in my book *Breaking the Threefold Demonic Cord*,[1] both divination and witchcraft move strongly with a Jezebel spirit: "[The python spirit] squeezes life out of hope, breakthroughs, finances and lives. . . . It is one way Jezebel locks us down into our past with no hope for freedom."

It is important to pay close attention to emotions at open doors or gates in dreams. If you feel fear, you may have to contend with an evil force before breakthrough comes.

- If a door opens and you have a sense of terror, it might indicate that the enemy is blocking your breakthrough. If you have a sense of choking during or after the dream, it is a clue that you may be contending against the python spirit.

- If you feel exhilaration and joy, this is a sign that break-through is occurring!

Dreams of Spiritual Warfare

We are all called to pray, but God has a specific purpose for giving warfare dreams and visions. The ultimate purpose is to inspire us with a revelation of our godly authority to defeat the enemy. In fact, it is even more important to remember that because of the cross Satan has *already* been defeated. Like the Israelites, however, we must still use our spiritual authority to drive the enemy out of our Promised Land.

Worship is a vital part of spiritual warfare, and many times the Lord is simply calling us to a time of worship and, therefore, leaving it up to Him to completely destroy our enemies. As we see in 2 Chronicles 20, Judah—which means "praise"—goes forth and "plows" in the spiritual realm of worship (see verses 21–22) and as a result defeats the plans of the devil. So whenever you get an opportunity to praise and worship Him, know that He is sending angels on assignment on your behalf at the same time!

Déjà Vu Dreams

Have you ever walked into a situation or place, or perhaps had a conversation with someone, and thought, *Wait a minute! I've been here before! This is weird, but I've had this talk before!* This is known as *déjà vu*, but I personally believe that it is con-firmation to you that God has been leading you by His Spirit . . . putting you at just the right place and time. So what really happened?

A quick review of Job 33:14–18 instructs us in the many ways God speaks—in dreams, in visions, when man is asleep:

"He opens the ears of men, and seals their instruction" (verse 16 NASB). When *déjà vu* occurs, it is as though God gave you a dream or vision and then "sealed" the instructions in that dream. He puts something in a plastic baggie and zips it shut until it is ready to be revealed (and used!).

If you are like me, you have woken from dreams just to almost forget them, even really awesome ones. I can tell the dream is leaving my remembrance—even if I write it down immediately!—and I think, *Where did that dream go?* Sometimes God takes it and zips it up in His baggie. In a *déjà vu* experience, He unzips it and unseals His mysteries. Dear one, this is an awesome sign from God that we are being led by His Spirit. Rejoice when this happens, for He is faithful. Remember, Job warns us that God *seals* their instructions "that He may turn man aside from his conduct, and keep man from pride" (verse 17 NASB). You may forget God's instruction for you until the time for it to be revealed . . . such as in a *déjà vu* experience. Again, we do not know our own hearts, so God is protecting us from the mystery of a dream or the instructions therein until we can properly handle it. These types of dreams (mysteries) keep us from pride.

It is all too true: Only through humility can we seek the hidden meanings that are sealed up until the appointed time of revelation. I cannot begin to tell you just how many "this is that" experiences I have had: I dreamed about something, forgot it and later experienced a portion of it, and it hit me—*This is that which I dreamed!* . . . Déjà vu.

Dreams with Impartation

I take great delight in impartation dreams because of how encouraging and empowering they are. Through impartation dreams (and visions) comes an activation of the gifts of the Spirit, as well as impartations of courage, emotional strength, passion, vision . . . and more! I have heard testimonies of others receiving an impartation of the gift of healing during the heavenly encounters of dreams and visions.

While I was writing this book, I had the most amazing dream . . . and a much needed one! I had been praying, while writing, that the Lord would speak to me concerning His hidden mysteries that come forth in His divine dream language. He confirmed in a dream that He would continue to give me revelation . . . even revelation that is presented in this book!

On that night I fell asleep completely overwhelmed and exhausted. I had been battling a rare form of vertigo and could not find a doctor who could properly diagnose my situation. I prayed before I fell asleep that I might receive some direction from the Lord so that I could be healed. During my sleep time, the Lord answered me powerfully in a dream.

Impartation dream of revelation. There was a knock at our door. I arose and looked as the door opened. Two angels approached me, dressed in white. They were beautiful, and the glory around them released a shimmery reflection as they walked toward me. In their hands each held a gift. They held out their hands to give the gifts to me, and then I awoke.

I was excited! I knew that God sent the angels with gifts of healing for me through a divine impartation. My faith arose and I was supernaturally empowered by the Lord to keep pursuing my healing and see it manifest.

Dear one, I am learning to receive impartations and then walk in them. I received an impartation to see my new season of healing, as well as the impartation to seek out what is hidden and discover the mysteries of heaven! God wants to minister to you, also. Have faith *now* to receive an impartation for all that God has for you, as you continue to dream dreams and have visions!

6

Other Common
Destiny Dreams

*A*s you can see, there are many types of dreams! I bet you are almost overwhelmed with all the information you are taking in . . . maybe even feeling *overloaded*. I can relate . . . I once believed I had to remember *all* categories of dreams and visions and the differences between them, and more besides. This is not as important as I thought! Do not worry too much about getting everything in the right category; above all, try to *keep it simple*.

In their insightful book *When God Speaks*, Chuck Pierce and Rebecca Sytsema explain that there are basically just three dream types. Their revelation has been extremely helpful for me as I interpret dreams, especially when I go on overload:

1. **A simple message dream.** In Matthew 1–2, Joseph understood the dreams concerning Mary and Herod. There was no real need for interpretation.

2. **A simple symbolic dream.** Dreams can be filled with symbols. Oftentimes the symbolism is clear enough that

the dreamer and others can understand it without any complicated interpretation. For instance, when Joseph had his dream in Genesis 37, he fully understood it, as did his brothers, to the point that they wanted to kill him, even though it has symbols of the sun, moon and stars.

3. **The complex symbolic dream.** This type of dream needs interpretative skill from someone who has unusual ability in the gift of interpretation or from someone who knows how to seek God to find revelation. We find this type of dream in the life of Joseph, when he interpreted Pharaoh's dream. In Daniel 2 and 4, we find some good examples of this type of dream. In Daniel 8, we find a dream in which Daniel actually sought divine interpretation.[1]

I have realized that I am not to fret over dream interpretation. It takes much patience and training by the Holy Spirit to learn how to do it. Plus, as I have stated, everyone needs to develop his/her own intimate language with God. Even though I am providing lists of symbols that have proven helpful, we are never to depend on someone else's revelation. A person's dream language is private, personal and intimate. The Holy Spirit is our main teacher. Other teachers and instructors provide help, but eventually we must hear from the Lord ourselves! This is all part of our discovery and Spirit-led journey. Do not rely on books—even this book—or charts of symbols and types as your ultimate source of understanding God's heavenly language. When you feel overwhelmed, as I often do, relax . . . breathe deep . . . and tell God, *I'll keep searching, but ultimately You have to lead me and guide me through this interpretation.* God is faithful; He will lead you into the understanding of what He has to say to you! Keep reading—there is much more to learn concerning God's voice through dreams and visions.

Dreams of Your House

Though I am not listing types of dreams in order of importance, I and numerous others concur that dreams about one's house are in the top five most *common* types of dreams.

The house normally represents an individual's life. Different circumstances taking place within the house represent the various activities in the life of the dreamer (and, at times, the lives of others as well). Dreams about your house can also represent your place of worship or the "house of God" that you attend. Sometimes a house can represent your mind as a "house of thoughts." These thoughts might represent the need for one to renew the mind as different strongholds are torn down and replaced with the Word of God.

- When documenting these types of dreams, try to recall the condition of the house: Does it need repair? Is the paint peeling? Is raw wood exposed, or do you see drywall underneath torn wallpaper? This could be a sign that the dreamer's life is being exposed and that his or her life needs to be repaired by the Lord. At times, dreams of a house in bad condition are directive dreams exhorting the dreamer to get spiritual guidance and counseling.

- Make note of the different rooms in the house: Each may represent a very specific event or thing. For instance, dreams of a bedroom could imply that intimacy with the Lord is needed. Dreaming of a bathroom may represent a needed washing with the Word of God or a cleansing from bad habits or hindrances. Dreaming of a kitchen could mean that God wants to feed you or that He is preparing a new "diet." The kitchen table may speak of God preparing a table in the midst of your enemies, or of you needing to eat at the Lord's table. If a dreamer is dreaming of the family room, it might indicate that God is doing something special within the family, such as healing the family of pain or trauma or bringing restoration.

- For many individuals, troubling events occurred in childhood in specific rooms or settings. A dreamer may dream of such a place and awake frightened, ashamed or even terrified. This is an indication that the Lord desires to heal a wound and/or memory. Destiny dreams can expose, but they are ultimately meant to get us moving into our destiny. On the other hand, dreaming of certain rooms can bring hope and joy, such as a family room decked for Christmas. Christmas trees often represent the impartation of gifts of the Holy Spirit; a dream of this nature would therefore be considered encouraging.

I remember a dream I had when I was thirty years old. At that time I was a mess. My life was a mess, my marriage was a mess and it seemed as if I messed up everything I attempted to do. One night, in desperation, I cried out to the Lord for help. I fell asleep immediately after praying, and He spoke to me in a dream.

Dream of my attic. I was in the attic of our home. There was wallpaper in the attic (I know, this is unusual . . . people do not wallpaper their attics!), and in some places it was torn off or peeling away from the drywall. Exposed drywall was everywhere.

I found a very old chest, what I would call a "hope chest." The chest had a huge padlock that kept it sealed. I knew that if I could find the key to the lock, I would find hope once again. I began to search everywhere—inside every storage box, behind old furniture . . . and then I saw the key! It was sticking out from under the wallpaper and exposed drywall.

I knew that the secrets I had been hiding from others must be shared so that I could be healed. My key to finding hope was directly connected to exposing areas of my life that I felt were shameful. I understood that, to be healed and delivered of my "mess," I had to share with someone my shame . . . and my pain . . . which I began to do.

This dream was the first step toward freedom. Did you notice the *hope* chest? My hope of being delivered was locked up, and the key to getting it unlocked was exposure. I had put up wallpaper to cover my mistakes, feelings, emotions and all that was wrong with me long enough . . . it was my destined time to have hope again and experience abundant life in Christ!

Dreams of Angels

Just as in biblical times, angels are very present in our dreams today. Whenever we dream of angels, it is symbolic of God's divine intervention. Angels are messengers, so, whether they appear in a dream or a vision, they always carry with them a message. They are sent to protect, come alongside us in destiny and help direct us in life.

I have most often seen angels in my dreams, but sometimes I see them in visions, also, in my mind's eye. I will never forget the Lord speaking to me during one vision in which a very large angel appeared to me. The Lord said, *Sandie, I send angels for a reason. Whenever they appear, ask Me why I sent them and what message they are bringing.* From that point forward I have always asked Him those questions, and what I found is that the message always brought glory to the Father. Angels are not God, they are messengers—and they are not to be worshiped! It saddens me to see people fall into this trap, which is strongly forbidden by the Word.

An angelic dream. I have had several dreams in which the angel Gabriel appeared to me bringing a very directional word from the Lord. I have always awakened from these dreams refreshed, encouraged and hopeful. It is always clear that God sent Gabriel for a specific reason, and heaven knows I have needed angelic intervention many times in my life!

In one dream, Gabriel said, "Sandie, it's important that before the church service you blow the *shofar*. Do this as the Spirit of God quickens you. When you do this, it will release the hosts of heaven to go forth and do battle on your behalf."

When I awoke from this dream, I was tremendously excited. I knew how the *shofar* was used by Israel to gather troops for warfare, so I was completely aware of its biblical significance. To this day, when the Lord quickens me, we blow the *shofar*, and the entire congregation is charged with faith in God.

Dreams of Correction

Corrective dreams directly target and expose the issues of our hearts. I could easily write a personal list of issues that I deal with . . . you might have a list as well . . . well, actually, we *all* do! When God intervenes in our night seasons with dreams about our issues, do we listen? This is why His night voice is so valuable—He chooses a time to speak truths to us knowing *we can't talk back!* It is easy to get comfortable with where we are in life, but God loves to smash our comfort zones and call us up higher. Why? Because He loves us and knows how much more He placed in us for us to reach.

I have certainly tried to ignore correctional dreams. But God's love for Sandie Freed keeps pursuing my heart, because He wants me completely free. I am positive that He has dealt with my character issues during dreams, issues of integrity and being honest and fair with others. My need for repentance is revealed to me during correctional dreams.

Dreams of Births/Babies

Dreams of births are usually not literal dreams about someone being pregnant or birthing a baby. (But nothing is always!) Most often they symbolize a new calling, a new season or a new gift, purpose or ministry coming forth in the life of the dreamer. The dream can be interpreted as someone giving birth to "vision." It can also symbolize the beginning of something new or a new season.

Dreams of births could be considered a type of destiny dream if God has a new adventure planned for your life. Sometimes they represent something (ministry, business, family) in infancy or early stages. Pay attention when documenting the dream whether the baby was given a name. If it was, then a good Internet search on the name would come in very handy for interpretation. For instance, a baby named Jacob could represent a new season in which one experiences a "name change" (a type of transformation), just as Jacob received when the Lord called him "Israel."

- Emotions and setting are extremely important when dreaming of babies. Carefully examine the setting: Is the baby in a crib? A play pen? Is someone holding the baby? If you are holding the baby or birthing it, you are the main one carrying the vision. If someone else is holding the baby (vision, ministry, etc.), then you may be sharing responsibility with another.

Dreams of Being Chased or Chasing

Chasing dreams are very common. In fact, I had dreams of being chased many times before I experienced various deliverances. These dreams most often represent enemies coming against your life and purpose. Enemies will almost always generate some level of fear in our lives, whether they oppose us in the natural realm or the spiritual one. Therefore, if fear is a stronghold in your life, the Lord may give you these dreams as a heads up for future deliverance from fear.

Things to note while documenting these types of dreams:

- Running dreams often bring a variety of emotions. Fear, anxiety and dread speak of running in fear from enemies, negative emotions, etc. On the other hand, joy, exhilaration, even hunger could represent a passionate pursuit (chasing) for His presence. Think about a childhood game of "tag-you're-it." That would be a fun type of chasing dream. Remember, nothing is always—most revelation from God is birthed out of intimacy, so the more time we spend with Him, the more He empowers us with greater understanding of our dreams!

Dreams of Dying

Most of the time dreams of dying are *not literal* but symbolic, representing something passing away or departing from the dreamer's life. Very often they represent dying to an old season or desire.

- Note once again who is dying in the dream and what that person means to the dreamer. The person in the dream may reveal a job ending, a career ending or perhaps a ministry season drawing to a close.
- Make note of the colors in the dream. If the dream is in black and white, it could be demonically inspired to cause fear and torment. If you see a lot of beautiful color, then something may be removed for a season, but resurrection and great breakthrough are coming!
- Since nothing is always when it comes to dream interpretation, these dreams can be literal. It is possible that the

Lord is putting it on your heart to pray for the person in the dream, specifically against premature death, sickness, disease, accidents, etc.

Dreams of Falling

Falling dreams reveal most often the fear of losing control. On a positive note, they can mean that someone is becoming free from a hindrance, burden, stronghold, even an addiction that is controlling him or her.

Many people with control issues have this type of dream. It is the Lord's desire that we completely put our trust in Him rather than things, people, jobs, the economy, etc. (see Proverbs 3:5). If we lack trust, He may allow dreams like these. I have had many dreams in which I am falling down and cannot get back up! Since I was a complete control freak, I was always falling down in my dreams. God was saying that I was unable to remain in control and that I was completely dependent on Him to pick me up, dust me off, and set me straight.

- Make note of the results of the fall. Was there pain, or was there a sense of freedom? Did you feel that you had "fallen" into sin?
- Since nothing is always, let's remember what Scripture states concerning falling: Psalm 116:8 and Psalm 56:13 talk about how God keeps our feet from falling (divine protection). Psalm 95:6 exhorts us to fall on our knees and worship the Lord our maker.

Ultimately, the interpretation begins with your emotion in the dream. Do you feel powerful? Do you have peace? Do you feel reverence? Is the enemy lying to you that you have "fallen from grace"? If so, examine your heart and life, repent from any sin and realize that you never really fall *from* grace but rather *into* grace! Dear ones, God *is* grace. *Run to Him and not from Him.* Dreams are not given from above to bring condemnation. The devil, however, can make suggestions that trouble our souls and, therefore, influence our dreams.

Dreams of Wild Animals

The most common dreams of wild animals are about snakes, which reveal Satan the serpent—the devil and his demonic forces working through lies and false accusations. Alligators indicate that someone of great influence has launched a demonic verbal attack with vicious gossip. In Scripture, the name Leviathan is another name for Satan (see Psalm 74:14; Job 3:8; 41:1; Isaiah 27:1). It symbolizes something hidden and dangerous—twisted conversations. It also represents the king of pride, which is, again, Satan.

Spiders represent being trapped in an evil web through something in which the dreamer is involved. Spiders also are symbolic of divination and witchcraft. Many dreamers have dreams about wolves and bears. Wolves can represent something wild and evil (the untamed nature and works of the flesh), and bears can represent a variety of things—being preyed upon, evil, Russia, judgment, anger or bitterness.

- If you dream about a snake and you are *not* afraid, it is possible that you have a "pet" snake—or a sin that you are "petting"! If there is fear, however, it probably means the enemy has targeted you and the Lord is exposing his evil plans. (For more on snakes, please refer to chapter 9.)
- Dragons are prevalent in many dreams. They are connected to the Leviathan spirit as well as witchcraft assignments. Be sure to use your discernment if these are prevailing so that you can pray accordingly.

Dreams of Domesticated Animals

It is very common for dreamers to dream of their domesticated animals, dogs and then cats being the most dreamed about. Dogs usually represent loyalty, companionship and protection. Try to remember the actions of a dog who was biting, growling or attacking. These types of actions may represent a friend who is about to betray you.

> **Dreams about Precious.** I used to have a lovely Yorkie named Precious, and I have had numerous dreams about her. I dreamed of her drowning in our backyard pool, so I would go outside with her every day to be sure she would not drown. I had dreams of her breaking our sliding glass door and coming out just fine on the other side. Naturally I would close the drapes to the door to keep her away. Once I dreamed of Precious wearing a priestly garment. It seemed weird at the time, and when I awoke I had no clue what it meant.

Actually, none of these dreams was literal. I realized later that many "precious" things in my life were being addressed by the Holy Spirit. The dream of her drowning meant that God was going to drown out anything more precious to me than He was! And the glass door . . . well, this really was a love pat from God. The dream was speaking to me about my precious seer gift that God had given me, to see through closed doors and to see future breakthroughs that awaited!

And, in the theme that nothing is always . . . I was shopping for groceries (I know, how spiritual is that?!) when the Lord spoke to me about Precious in the priestly garment. He said it was related to Psalm 133, about how good and pleasant it is for the saints to be in unity, for it is like "precious" oil poured over the head of the priesthood. I knew the Lord was speaking to me concerning the importance of unity.

- Animals mean different things to different people. To me a Doberman pinscher represents fear; to someone else it might mean protection. Continually rely on the guidance of the Holy Spirit when interpreting these types of dreams.
- Pets' names are important in a dream, just as people's names are. Consider the meanings of the names when interpreting.

Dreams in the Natural

So far we have discussed dreams and visions we receive from the Holy Spirit. There are, however, dreams that originate completely in the soul of the natural man. Reader, please remember this—*not all dreams are from God!* Many times we have dreams that are not supernatural but rather are influenced by daily activities, chemicals/drugs and issues of our souls. An example is someone who is very ill having a dream about being ill. In no way should this be interpreted to mean that God's will is for the illness to remain, or that this person is destined to be ill until death. It is simply the body influencing the dream world. Another example is having a bathroom dream simply for the natural reason of needing to go to the bathroom at that time.

Sometimes when we fall asleep, our minds have been running wild with thoughts. Disappointments, frustrations, confrontations, anger . . . all of these can influence our sleep. We may have dreams about the cares of the day, but this does not mean that the dream is from God. Ecclesiastes 5:3 states, "A dream comes when there are many cares." Dreaming is a way for our minds to process our thoughts and emotions and does not necessarily mean God is speaking!

In the same way, not all visions are from God. Some inner visions are simply the product of our imaginations or hopeful thinking. I like what Jane Hamon says in her book *Dreams and Visions*:

Natural dreams and visions are not produced by the Spirit of God but by the soul—the mind, will and emotions. Because the images originate in the soul, they give insight into what is affecting us both consciously and unconsciously.[2]

As an example, Jane explains how a man named Elias Howe had a dream that helped him solve a problem while inventing the sewing machine. While he was puzzling over his machine design, an answer came from within his own intellect through a dream. This is a great example of something needed in the natural being reflected in our world of dreams.

Dreams from the Demonic Realm

Another source of dreams that cannot go unmentioned is the demonic realm. It is very true that anything the Lord uses to bless us and empower us, the enemy is bent on invading and stealing. Dreams from the demonic realm are referred to by many as "dark dreams" and are usually identified by the darkness of their tone. Sadness, grief, extreme depression, fear, anxiety, suicidal tendencies and extreme melancholy are characteristic of these dreams. The feelings of these dark emotions linger upon awakening.

Demonic dreams are usually in black and white, without color. Nothing is always, but that is the rule of thumb. I have also had dreams from God that were in black and white, which meant to me that they were prophetic—black and white, plain and simple. These are instruction to look at the dream from a prophetic perspective. I always keep in mind, however, that most such dreams are demonic in nature.

Black, gray, muted colors and a sickly color of green are also characteristics of demonic dreams. Keep this in mind while interpreting your dreams. God is a God of color. A rainbow full of color surrounds His throne! Since God is light, the lack of light (expressed in muted colors, grays, etc.) speaks of the lack of His light—hence, the demonic realm.

False Dreams

False dreams are meant to establish ungodly principles and lifestyles. As a pastor for many years, I have sadly witnessed many of God's children receiving and being misled by false dreams. Let me give you an example: A man in our church had a dream that he was married to a woman in our congregation. Problem was, she was already married! A second problem was that *he* was already married to someone else, too. Unfortunately, he told the woman his dream (never do that!) and persuaded her to believe the dream was from God. Even though I counseled against this interpretation and explained it was a false dream, they each divorced their spouses and married. Today they are divorced from each other! They were both miserable after their divorces, and, as a result, she became abused and he became an alcoholic.

Dark Dreams

Dark dreams are foreboding in mood, with dark and muted colors. Dreams with sickly green colors and shades can be discerned as demonic in nature. Take a moment and reflect on some of your dreams. Did you make note of the colors? Most dreams are full of color—and those colorful dreams are mostly from the Holy Spirit. Black and white dreams are considered mainly from the demonic realm.

My dark dream. One night I awoke from a dream feeling extremely fearful—as if someone had literally sucker punched me! I shook with an overwhelming sense of foreboding. As I began to write down the dream, I recalled dark, gray figures reaching out to grab me—I knew they were evil and

118

meant to harm . . . maybe even to kill me. Then I noticed that they had very long, black tongues.

As I asked the Holy Spirit about this dream, it occurred to me that the entire dream—its tone, color and message—was dark. I understood that the enemy was attempting to snatch away my destiny, if I believed his evil lies concerning my future. And therein lay the message: *Do not listen to lies from the source of evil.*

The very next day I received devastating news that someone close to me was misrepresenting me and spreading lies about me. The dream immediately came to mind, and right then I chose not to allow any negative words to distract me; I was not going to believe the lie of the enemy, who was falsely accusing me and insisting that my reputation was ruined. I knew that I had to trust the Lord to preserve my reputation and that He would protect me and my integrity through this fiery trial.

Nightmares

Nightmares are dreams that cause fear and panic. Many nightmares are the result of trauma, but they are also connected to the demonic realm. They are very common for children and new believers. Unbelievers have nightmares, too, and it is possible that the Lord uses even these dreams to reach out to dreamers and expose their hearts and/or fears. Not all nightmares, then, are from the devil.

As a definition, nightmares are dreams (and, at times, visions) that cause panic, fear or anxiety. Many times they are considered "wake-up dreams" because they cause the dreamer to wake up out of sleep. These occurrences place the dreamer in urgent situations of apparent danger, physically and/or psychologically.

Nightmares can be caused by the enemy for the purpose of intimidation and to induce fear. (Nightmares open the door for other fears, such as fear of rejection and fear of failure.)

These dreams often reveal generational strongholds (enemies) at work that need to be cut off. Though I discuss nightmares more later, for now it is enough to say that nightmares are frightening, intimidating and can affect us for years . . . even into adulthood!

Since nothing is always, I have to mention this: God is always in control of our lives. I have realized that many of my nightmares opened the door to a greater understanding of the many strongholds that were negatively affecting my life. God will use everything—even nightmares—and work it together for our good. Nightmares expose the enemy on all counts!

- In your dream, do you recall the backdrop? Was there a house or a particular room? Were others in the dream besides you? (These could indicate a time/place of earlier trauma, which the enemy uses to torment a person in nightmares.)
- Have you anointed your room with oil since having nightmares? *This is important!* Anoint the threshold and door of the room in which you sleep to draw a spiritual line forbidding the enemy to visit you (or anyone else) through nightmares.

Lucid Dreaming

Nightmares do not have to continue to terrorize us and/or our children. As I discuss in chapter 13, the Lord empowers us through nightmares to exercise our spiritual authority and rebuke the enemy and his plans while we are still dreaming! In a lucid dream you are made aware that you can actively overcome the wicked plans of Satan. You can even wake up, think over the dream, fall back asleep into the dream and, while still dreaming, defeat him. Through practice you can wake yourself up if you do not like the story line in the dream. This takes perseverance and much practice, but a dreamer can become an active participant in his or her own dream and make quality decisions that affect the dream's outcome. (This is not new science; the understanding of this has been around for more than a century.)

> **An example of lucid dreaming.** Once I had a nightmare in which three different women operating in a Jezebel spirit were riding in my car. For me, when I dream about my car, it almost always refers to my anointing. Each of the women was attempting to control and manipulate me. In the dream, I became anxious, confused and deathly ill. It was clear that a Jezebel spirit had targeted my prophetic anointing. I awoke from the dream and began to tell the Lord how much I did not want those women in my car! While I was pondering this more, the Lord said, *Well, take spiritual authority and command them to get out!* I fell back asleep and went immediately back into my dream. I pointed my finger at each of them and said, "Get out of my car, don't touch my anointing and leave now in Jesus' name!" And guess what—they left!

It is important to empower our children with this spiritual skill, too, so pay close attention when I write about lucid dreams and children's nightmares, and how to help your child in those experiences, in chapter 13. Asking the Holy Spirit to reveal the source of the nightmare is always important. The enemy attempts to terrorize us and our children to steal our destinies. Fear paralyzes us, and, therefore, nightmares can easily be discerned as a tactic of the enemy.

We have covered a large number of dream types and themes, which should enable you to begin to recognize the different settings God uses to communicate with you in the night seasons. Now it is time to turn our attention to an even more involved aspect of dream interpretation—understanding symbolism.

7

Understanding Symbolism

*I*n a previous chapter, you read about dreams and visions
containing mysteries and hidden meanings embedded
in dream symbolism—and that it is our privilege, our honor,
to search them out. All through Scripture we can see that God
speaks in symbolism. And because dreams are very often an
expression of our own emotions, much symbolism is involved.
As children of God, we are each on a journey to discover the
interpretations of our dreams, first through Scripture and then
from the backdrop of our own lives.

Now it is time to get down to some basic understanding of
how to interpret dream symbolism. First and foremost in this
effort is a principle we get from Scripture, the "law of first mention." It is foundational to biblical interpretation, and it simply
means that how a word, image or symbol was used in its very
first appearance in Scripture is a key to how it should be interpreted today. A symbol and its interpretation can change from
dream to dream, yet the law of first mention is a consistency in
symbolic language that cannot ever be overlooked.

The Lord brought me a great victory through this law, using a revelation about the meaning of the number seven. Seven is often a symbol of God's completeness. If we study the seventh day of creation in Genesis, we notice that God *rested* on that day. The completion of His work of creation resulted in rest, and the number seven in Scripture is many times a symbol of rest and completion. But, reader, hang in there with me—there is more! This revelation will empower you.

Hebrews 3:11 reveals that what the children of Israel were seeking in their Promised Land was rest. Their entrance into the place of promise foreshadowed our entering into the rest provided in Christ's finished work at the cross. If we study the four gospels combined, we notice that Jesus declared seven times, "It is finished!" Therefore, the idea of rest—symbolized in the number seven—is connected to God's completion of something . . . ultimately the finished work of Christ at the cross.

This means a lot for dream interpretation. If we dream of the number seven, God might be telling us to cease from the works of the flesh, to stop striving and accept the righteous standing that Christ accomplished on our behalf. To me, this revelation was huge! I was a performer, a people pleaser, and I believed (falsely) that I had to be righteous in my own strength and merit. When I received this revelation—that only through Christ's accomplishments at the cross was I righteous—it set me free from all religious performance!

I have had many dreams of seven beds. That is all. Just seven beds in a large room. Before I understood dream symbolism, I thought the beds meant that I needed bed rest. This is because I had a premature death assignment from the enemy, and he has targeted me often with deadly viruses. It took some time for me to press past my fears of death. The dreams of seven beds were given to me several times until I finally understood that the Lord had a Sabbath rest for me. I was a perfectionist to the max. My testimony is about me trying to be good enough or perfect enough so God would deliver me from death assignments and equip me to walk in total freedom from fear and anxiety. Over a season, I learned that He alone is my land of rest. God has promised me a Promised Land—that is true. But ultimately, I had to rest in the fact that He had already accomplished all I needed at the cross. I have had to learn to rest in His completed work.

There is also a law of first mention to *you*! Whenever God begins to speak revelation to you, He will introduce first words, symbols or images, which become a pattern or foundation on which to build for future interpretation. Once these are introduced into your spiritual vocabulary, they will have consistent meanings for you. Let's say you dream about your pet, and you discern the Holy Spirit is speaking to you about "precious things." After all, many of us have pets that are precious to our hearts. Once the image of your pet has entered into your spiritual vocabulary as a symbol for precious things, you can be more confident in interpretation: The dream has something to do with things that are precious to you. Most of the time God is very consistent with His revelatory symbolism; keep in mind, though, that *nothing is always* in dream interpretation. Be ready to discover more even when you encounter a familiar symbol in the dream.

Tools for Dream Interpretation

Simply by journaling, asking yourself the right questions and remembering details of the dream before they are forgotten, you will have most of what you need to interpret dreams. The following steps will help you lay out the framework of your dream to help clarify its meaning.

1. Keep It Simple

I always encourage my dream interpretation students to *keep it simple*. To start with, we must try to reduce every dream (and vision) to its simplest form and use that as a foundation on which to build. Therefore, when you write your dream, try to make it simple and try to *keep the main thing the main thing.* Sometimes dreams have a lot of detail, but much of the detail is not necessary in dream interpretation. In fact, too many details will muddy the interpretation.

2. Consider the Context

We need to prayerfully consider the context of the dream. Determine what the dream is mainly about; once you have finalized its content, you will be able to discern which direction is required for interpretation. This is important because words and images can have several different meanings. The lion, for example, is used symbolically in the Bible in different ways. Jesus is referred to as the Lion of the tribe of Judah in Revelation 5:5. When the context of a dream points in this direction, you should consider the attributes of royalty, strength, kingship, courage and boldness. Because you are created in His image, perhaps God is reminding you that you have these same qualities. (See Revelation 5:5; Judges 14:18; 2 Samuel 1:23;17:10; Genesis 49:9; Numbers 24:9; Hosea 13:8.) That would be an awesome dream!

On the other hand, a lion can represent an evil person or demonic assignment. In 1 Peter 5:8 (NKJV), Peter describes the devil as a "roaring lion, seeking whom he may devour." If, in a dream, the lion appears to be evil, one might interpret it as a time to be vigilant and on the lookout for a demonic attack. The overall context will help you determine which way to pray.

3. Determine if a Dream Is Recurring

We discussed recurring themes in dreams earlier, but allow me to elaborate on both *repeated* dreams and *recurring* dreams. A repeated dream is given for several reasons:

- In previous interpretations, you missed a particular divine insight.
- You misunderstood the message within the dream.
- You had an improper response to the dream.

Dreams that recur are repeated more than twice over a period of time. These often indicate an issue that needs to be resolved:

- You are harboring unforgiveness toward someone.
- There are unhealed hurts or wounds from your past.
- Strongholds need to be dealt with and pulled down.
- Generational strongholds of iniquity, poverty, infirmity, etc. need to be revealed and pulled down.
- You have an ongoing misunderstanding or partial understanding from a message given in a particular dream.
- You had an improper response to your previous dreams.

Sometimes you may have the same dream multiple times in the same night. You will often notice that it is actually the same dream in a different format. This means there are several ways to look at the context, but all have the same conclusion. If you have repetitive dreams, continue to look for a central theme or a common thread when seeking interpretation. Once a repetitive dream is properly acted on, you will probably notice the dream will discontinue. This is a good sign that you have heard from the Lord and you have yielded yourself to His directives.

4. Evaluate the Full Picture

You must take some time to evaluate the full picture—this is key in dream interpretation. Ask yourself, *Am I the main person in the dream, or am I observing?* If you are observing in the overall setting, most likely the dream is not primarily about you. It is probably about someone else or even another place or event. If you are an observer, then you are "witnessing" an occurrence that God desires a witness for. You might think this a little odd if you have never been told to examine your dreams this way. This is because we have thought that *all* dreams are primarily about *us*. This is not so. God shows us things concerning others at times, and I feel this is healthy, as we are to pray for each other and not be overly self-focused and introspective.

In several Scriptures God teaches us about the need for two or three witnesses. One is in Matthew 18:16, which instructs us to take two or three witnesses when approaching someone who needs truth spoken but refuses to hear. In a case like this, you may be a witness and called to pray and/or intercede for someone God is trying to reach. Another Scripture is Matthew 18:20, in which Jesus describes the power of agreement. He states that whenever two or three are gathered together in His name, He is in their midst! Therefore, in your dream, you may be a witness called to agree with something being revealed in the dream. That is exciting! You are being used to witness and agree with the will of God . . . in a dream!

5. Determine Your Role

If you are not merely observing, are you a participant in the dream? Your participation may reflect your love, concern and desire to be a part of a person's life who is in the dream. If so, that could be a prayer assignment. If you are still not the main focus, however, the dream is most likely not about you.

6. Determine the Focus

Are *you* the main focus in the dream? Are all the people in the dream talking to you, centered on your needs and focused on you? If so, try to recall where you were in the dream. A kitchen, a bedroom, outside in a garden, in the bathroom? These will help determine the message in the dream.

128

7. *Pay Attention to Emotions*

I cannot say this enough: Try to recall your thoughts, feelings and emotions in the dream. Were you fearful, happy, remorseful? You will need to make note of emotions such as anger, resentment and/or emotional pain. Did you talk in the dream, and, if so, what words were exchanged? Did you awake from the dream with dread and fear or joy and excitement? God will often highlight a particular emotion so that it can be addressed. You will know by your discernment and intuition what the most important emotions are, so do not worry or fret over it. The Lord knows how to redirect us if our interpretations are not correct.

Ways to Keep Interpretation Simple

When heaven touches the dream world, it is a most exciting journey. Hearing God's voice, directives and, yes, correctives never ceases to excite me! This is because I, like you, long to know His heart for my life and to make a shift in that direction. Understanding and interpreting the myriad of symbols within a dream, however, is a complex and at times confusing process. Therefore, I want to take a moment to review what you have learned to this point so that the interpretation process appears more precise and simple:

1. Not all dreams are from God.
2. Most dreams are not to be taken literally and need interpretation.
3. The Holy Spirit is the ultimate guide and teacher of proper interpretation.
4. Dreams are always to be considered on a personal basis first, rather than assuming the dream is about someone else.
5. God will often speak in familiar terms. He will even use your own phrases and jokes.

6. Always write down your dream upon awakening. A dream journal gives a central place for recording. Give the dream a title and a date.

7. Take time to ponder your dream and allow the Holy Spirit to lead you. Do not rush the interpretation.

8. Reduce your dream to the simplest form—keep the main thing the main thing! Ask yourself if there is a central theme. Is a main thought, issue or particular word mentioned several times?

9. Take note of how you felt when you awoke—angry, fearful, excited?

10. Note if you had a nightmare or awoke to an evil presence in the room. This could have been a demonic dream.

11. Awakening from a dream to a heavenly atmosphere often indicates that an angel brought a dream to you and the angelic presence is still abiding.

12. Consecutive dreams often connect similar meanings. God frequently speaks the same message in different ways and with different symbolism.

13. Note the colors in the dream. Is the dream completely in black and white or in vivid colors, such as green and red? Note the main color throughout the dream.

14. Is there more than one theme in the dream? Quite often God will give several themes in one dream.

15. Many dreams are for the future and can only be understood as they unfold over a period of time. Again, do not rush the interpretation. Patience is a virtue in dream interpretation.

16. Dreams may be for you personally or to guide you in prayer and intercession for church, city, national and international issues.

17. Ask! Ask! And ask again! Dream interpretation comes from asking God for answers.

Sources for Symbolic Interpretations

Because we see in part and know in part, we will always need to look beyond ourselves for help in interpreting messages from heaven, whether dreams or visions. God gives revelation to many of His children, so you should be aware that you will need to pull from several sources when interpreting dreams.

When we have a heavenly encounter and need to seek the interpretation, the very first place to look is *always* (I cannot stress this enough!) in Scripture. The Bible is full of symbolism in parables and allegories (as well as documented dreams and visions) from which we can draw types, shadows and symbols. Bread, for example, is often a metaphor for life, but it also points to Jesus Christ, as He is the Bread of Life. A door is another metaphor for Jesus Christ, as He is *the* door. A lamb can represent Jesus Christ, a sacrifice or even the need to follow the Shepherd. The mustard seed is a metaphor for faith . . . and on and on. As treasure hunters, we will need a long time to get to the end of all the symbols in the Bible!

In chapter 9 I have provided an A–Z dictionary of symbols that have become my personal revelation; when you need a quick reference, I believe this dictionary will empower you. It is not, however, and never will be intended to replace Scripture. Please do not allow any book, list or teaching to become your only guide to understanding something so vast as God's heavenly language! It can be dangerous for us to use any one source to interpret dreams—other than the Bible, of course. Because so many aspects of modern life are not found in the Bible, however, many teachers, authors and ministers have had to seek the Holy Spirit to understand modern symbolism. My dictionary, for example, includes symbols such as automobiles and airplanes.

A favorite book of mine for learning symbols and types— one that is completely scripturally based—is written by Kevin J. Conner: *Interpreting the Symbols and Types* (Bible Temple

Publishing, 1992). Other sources for symbolic interpretation are dictionaries, encyclopedias, the Internet, books of names with Scripture references—and do not forget about prayer! Do not hesitate to use various types of resources whenever you are considering interpretations. Remember, God at one time spoke through a donkey!

Interpreting Symbols in Dreams

Now that we have laid a good foundation, let's turn our attention to how to interpret specific symbols that appear in dreams. Again, the categories that appear in the next sections are not all-inclusive, but they will serve as a starting point as you get used to recognizing images in dreams as symbols and determining how to interpret them.

Colors

I have read in many different books and heard seminar speakers say that if someone dreams in black and white, it is *always* a demonic dream. But—as I am sure you have noticed—I strongly believe that *nothing is always*. I have had many godly dreams in black and white. Because I am a bottom-line, black-and-white person (meaning I am truth oriented, so I tell it like I see it), I have many dreams for which, upon awakening, I remember no colors at all. Yet I knew the dreams were from God. Also, I am very prophetic. To a degree, prophetic people are black-and-white, bottom-line people by nature. When I have colorless dreams, they are usually prophetic. Keep in mind that the context of the dream is the key, not necessarily the colors that appear. Still, colors in dreams are very important. I have provided an entire section in chapter 9 that includes my personal revelation concerning colors, as well as a biblical understanding.

Numbers

We have already discussed the significance of the number seven, but there is much more to understanding number symbolism in dreams. Yet another section of numerical interpretations, both biblical and numerical, appears in chapter 9. You will want to refer to this list often as you continue to interpret dreams and visions. Numbers are both factual and fascinating; they have always proven to be keys to unlocking much interpretation.

That is why it is very important, upon awakening, not only to try to remember if there were specific numbers in the dream but also to jot down the time you awoke. Many times I have awoken and looked at the clock to see the time was 3:33. I know from previous experience that when the Lord speaks to me in the form of three 3s, He is probably speaking to me about Jeremiah 33:3: "Call to me and I will answer you and tell you great and unsearchable things you do not know." That is confirmation that if I ask the Lord the meaning to my dream, He desires to reveal it to me! Yes, He truly loves it when we go on a treasure hunt with Him.

When you awake, notice the time, jot it down and then search your dream for other numbers; then pray and ask the Holy Spirit for the interpretation. Next, look through Scripture for biblical references with that number combination (such as Jeremiah 33:3 and Psalm 3:33). Keep in mind that combinations of numbers could be interpreted various ways—3:33 could indicate 3 plus 3 plus 3, which equals 9, meaning the number 9 is what God wants you to study more thoroughly. Then seek out other reference materials concerning biblical numerology for guidance in interpretation. You could also search the other references that I mentioned . . . but, most importantly, ask the Holy Spirit for guidance.

The number six is also full of symbolism; six is the number for man, for on the sixth day of creation, God created man. I believe it is also safe to conclude that day six is the day of man. Now, if we go from Genesis all the way to the last book of the Bible, we find that the number 666 is identified as the *number of a man* (see Revelation 13:18). Most believers are aware that 666 is also identified as the mark of the Beast, the Antichrist. Notice the *three* sixes? Three is the number that signifies the Trinity. Because 666 is the number for mankind, then, it represents a false trinity—the exaltation of man, mankind and humanism. Quite often six symbolizes the curse that came upon mankind in the Garden, as well. So the number six can represent a curse, a generational curse *or* mankind and the flesh.

Dreams about People

In chapter 5 we touched on dreams concerning our generations and dreams about past relationships. Since people are often symbols in our dreams, the subject deserves more discussion.

People that we know and love during our lifetimes play major roles in our dreams. God will also use the generations that came before us to reveal areas of demonic strongholds, blind spots, and maybe areas of sin that need repentance. To better understand what these people symbolize in your dreams, ask yourself these questions:

1. Do I know this person? How well?
2. What does this person do in life (occupation, parent, pastor, etc.)?
3. What is the person's name? Look up the meaning of the name in a names book with scriptural references and/or search for the meaning on the Internet.
4. What does this person symbolize to me (love, success, failure, control, manipulation, jealousy, competition, anger, etc.)?
5. What emotions rise up when I think about this person?

6. Are you in authority over this person, or is he/she in authority over you?

7. Using adjectives, how would you describe this person?

8. In the dream, was this person actually "acting out" how you would describe her/him?

9. Do you desire to have a specific relationship with this person? If so, describe.

God Gives Us Dreams of Hope

As I wrote earlier, one of the most significant reasons that I personally believe God gives us dreams and visions is for us to be edified, exhorted and comforted. Many times God will encourage us and give hope so that we can endure the race. When symbolism is meant to give us hope from God, the dream can be full of images such as doors opening, new paths being taken or boats and anchors, since Christ is our "anchor" of hope (see Hebrews 6:19).

Sometimes a dream confirms that we are on the right path and exhorts us to fight the good fight of faith. Other times, He may be revealing that someone besides you needs to be encouraged. Keep in mind that the complete revelation of a dream will come with time. It may take years for a full interpretation to come forth, but God will give you just enough to offer hope.

As you know, I have almost died several times in my life. Even after recovery from anorexia, I continued to battle the spirit of death. Part of the sickness that I dealt with included digestive disorders. The thought of returning to an old pattern of sickness and disease was frightening, and I asked the Lord to reveal what was happening to my body.

I fell asleep, and the Lord gave a dream that involved much symbolism that pointed the way to hope: I was searching for rock treasures in an open field. I realized that I had stepped on something because my foot began to sting, followed by a painful ache in my heel. Upon observing my foot, I realized a snake's head was smashed into my heel, with its fangs stuck in the bottom of my foot. (Obviously, I had stepped on the serpent's head!) I called for my husband to remove the snake's head, and we noticed that the head was so crushed into my heel the only way to remove it was to "peel" it away.

My heel began to have a dull pain, and I remembered that I had been through this experience before. The memory of that previous battle for my life was too fresh; it engulfed me like a shroud. In my dream I was cringing, thinking about having to go through this again. As my husband pulled back the fangs, I remembered this assignment of death, and I wondered if I would soon die because of the venom that was already in my system.

Suddenly, a medical journal flashed before my eyes. The journal opened to a specific chapter and page, which read, "This is a medical journal on how to treat a snake bite. This particular bite causes digestive disorders." The dream ended.

Clearly, I had my answer from the Lord! All of the physical and emotional discomfort I was experiencing was the result of a demonic assignment. It was not the result of poor eating habits or stress, and I was not going to die! Hallelujah! My faith arose within me, along with a fresh determination to fight the good fight of faith.

The Lord revealed this dream for encouragement. I was to continue looking for the treasures of His Kingdom, knowing He was protecting me. If I had not been given the dream, I would have attempted to change my diet or take various medications. The Lord was instructing me that I was to rise up in faith and fight the enemy.

In situations of uncertainty, we often need confirmation from the Lord. Confirmation brings us comfort, like a lamp unto our feet when we are blinded in the darkness.

Why Will God Not Speak Plainly?

Some of you may be asking why it appears so difficult to hear God's voice through dreams and visions. After all, God could simply send an angel to direct us, just as He did in the Old and New Testaments.

In this age of doubt and unbelief, I am not entirely positive that even an angel would get our attention. Our culture and false belief systems are contaminated with mindsets that inhibit supernatural manifestations. I have come to the understanding that God gives us dreams because He has to bypass our minds to speak to our spirits. If we consider the biblical account of Zacharias, we find that even when an angel visits a priest to give him the Word of the Lord, he may still doubt! Take a moment to read Luke 1:15–18, the biblical account of the angel Gabriel announcing to Zacharias that he would have a son who would bring revival to the sons of Israel. Keep in mind that this was a visitation from God that probably came in the form of a vision . . . and Zacharias basically argues with the messenger!

Dear one, it is time to listen once more! Due to his doubt and unbelief, Zacharias was struck dumb and was unable to speak until the day John the Baptist was circumcised. It is quite clear that, at times, God may have to shut our mouths to halt our negativity. So why does God not speak to us in plain speech? Because even an angelic visit that communicates the Word of the Lord may not be enough to keep us from questioning Him. Let me repeat this for significance: He may yet bypass our minds and speak to our spirits in a dream or vision, or else we might argue with Him and contaminate the prophesied seeds of revelation. And, knowing my history of doubt, I am glad He does!

Saints, we do not have control over what we dream. God simply "pops" a dream into our spirits, very similar to inserting a DVD into a DVD player. Sometimes He reveals areas that we do not want to see about ourselves and the future. Many of us, myself included, have "blind spots," things we are blinded to. God reveals hidden areas of our hearts, the inner motives that we would rather not see. He also reveals how we feel toward others in our hearts—jealousy, envy, competition and the like. By bypassing the mind, God goes right to the spirit. He speaks Spirit to spirit because He does not desire negative influences to override our faith. When we awake from dreams, we cannot arise and proclaim, "I made myself dream about this." We cannot make ourselves dream anything. This is one area over which we have *no* control, and this is probably why God chooses to use it!

You are doing great! Thank you for continuing this journey with me. Now let's discuss simple ways to document your dreams and a few keys to consider as you interpret them.

8

Applying Interpretation

*B*efore jumping into lists of symbols and their meanings, it is important to lay a bit more foundation. I know—I have been laying foundations throughout this entire book! But learning heaven's language is not unlike learning a foreign language; it can be quite complex, yet surprisingly simple. A strong foundation for interpreting symbols will make things clearer.

Like Learning a Foreign Language

I remember the struggles I had to learn Spanish. I had to force my tongue to make the most unusual sounds! At first, the new words do not "feel right"; it is difficult to enunciate each syllable, and it takes time and effort for the language to make sense when we are used to communicating in our native languages. It also takes time for our speech to make sense to *others*. (My Spanish teacher endured much affliction from my efforts!)

The same is true when experiencing and understanding this new language of God. It may seem foreign; His voice may not "sound right." He is speaking differently than before, and we do not fully comprehend the message. As a result, we cannot translate His meaning correctly. This is because the symbolic terms He often speaks in *are* foreign in the beginning; through time, effort, discernment and prayer, you will begin to understand this new vocabulary and acquire confidence in interpretation.

I wrote earlier about how Jesus spoke often in parables; this is another example of symbolism. He told stories of everyday life and events that the people could easily understand, though they symbolized something else. When He spoke of the leaven of the Pharisees, for example, He was describing their sin and deception overshadowing the truth. The disciples, however, thought that Jesus was speaking literally concerning leaven (or yeast)—yet the entire parable was symbolic. In other parables Jesus compared Himself to a vine, a door, a shepherd, bread and wine—all are examples of symbolism.

Symbolism is also used throughout the Psalms and Revelation. Psalm 18 is filled with vivid imagery depicting God's power and might: smoke rising from the nostrils of God, fire coming from His mouth, dark clouds underneath God's feet and shooting arrows (verses 8–9, 14). In Revelation 12, the apostle John records a picture of a lady in labor and a dragon poised to devour the child she will deliver. We know from studying the symbolism of this passage that the woman represents the Church, while the dragon represents the Antichrist. The passage refers to the process of the Church coming forth in power and authority; it is similar to a child in the natural being birthed through travail and labor. The dragon is a symbol of the antichrist spirit that constantly seeks to steal what God is birthing and devour the seed. There are many such examples of symbolism in Scripture, and if we could not understand God's language, we would not understand most of the Bible.

The Elementary Language

God has a unique way of using symbols with which we are already familiar. If I say the word *dog*, what do you picture? I hope you see a dog, but what type of dog? Small? Large? A terrier? A poodle? You probably have not thought of the word *dog* in this way, but it became a symbol of communication between me and you, bringing to your mind the image of a dog.

Though we often conclude that symbols may be difficult to understand, in reality they are quite elementary. When I was a teacher at the elementary level, I taught children to read using illustrations and pictures, which were merely symbols that represented words. In your memory, recall whether your first-grade teacher held a picture of a cat, for example, and asked you to repeat the word. I remember my teacher holding up the letters *C-A-T*; these letters were symbols of how the word *cat* should be spelled.

We understand God's symbolism the same way: Each symbol is a picture that represents a word or group of words. Road signs are basic examples of this. Most everyone recognizes the meanings of symbols representing stoplights, stop signs, railroad crossings and crosswalks. Other fundamental symbols are used in mathematics: plus (+) or minus (−) signs, multiplication (×) or percentage (%) signs, and one of the most popular signs, which never needs interpretation: the dollar sign ($$$$)! Doctors have easily recognizable emblems, certain church denominations have recognized symbols and policemen have badges of authority. There are too many to name. In the same way, each symbol in a dream carries a meaning.

Dreams are a universal language—there are dreamers all over the world from all nations and cultures. Because a symbol's basic characteristics are the same around the world, they are mostly universally interpreted the same way. We must never assume, however, that even universal symbolism always represents the same thing in every dream. Flags of countries, for example, are recognized as symbols representing nations and their governments, but to a dreamer a flag is still subject to individual interpretation. In China, the dragon is a national symbol; thus in dreams a Chinese flag may represent the dragon mentioned in Revelation 12 rather than the Chinese government. The symbol depends completely on the dreamer's understanding and personal dream vocabulary.

Scenes and Settings

Most often, God paints dreams on the canvas of your own life. Like an artist adding one color upon another, technique upon technique, the Lord does quite the same. He will build line upon line and precept upon precept through a dream or series of dreams, beginning with that which with we are familiar and adding new information to bring new revelation. He "draws a picture" for us to see and then empowers us with revelation to be transformed.

He sometimes gives dreams containing unfamiliar people. Unless you understand that they likely represent your life, you may not comprehend the intent behind your dream. In that way, dreams are similar to a snapshot. Have you observed a picture of someone you did not personally know? You probably cannot relate to that person. Actually, most often you would not care about someone you did not know in a picture. Many dreams are like that. We often dream of people we do not know and scenes we have never experienced. We must become committed to understanding the people, scenes and settings represented in the snapshot, for quite often the people in a picture reveal characteristics about us.

Have you noticed that when you get to know the people in a picture, it takes on a whole new meaning? Amazing, isn't it? It is the same with dreams. The more we get to know the symbols in the picture God is painting, the more we are interested in that picture! Time will train you in your ability to recognize the meaning of unfamiliar people and places painted on the backdrop of your own life.

Emotions and Dreams

Psychologists often have children express themselves by drawing pictures. A psychologist studies the drawings of these children by examining the symbolism in their illustrations, because deep-rooted emotions are expressed through the release of demonstrative art.

As a pastor, I often counsel families with emotionally damaged children. After consulting with professional counselors, I have come to understand that very often, when a child draws pictures, an emotion is conveyed through symbols in them. The counselors explain, for example, that pictures of a child with a bandaged limb many times symbolize some type of abusive situation; a drawing of a home with only one parent often represents divorce or fears of divorce. Children have drawn pictures of themselves with unhappy faces or frowns to symbolize their unhappiness. These are only some examples of natural emotions expressed through symbolism that can also be conveyed through symbols in dreams.

If you experience emotion within a dream, much of the time the emotion is an expression of a real emotion you are dealing with in everyday life. Upon awakening from an emotional dream, allow the Holy Spirit to guide you concerning a pent-up emotion or an emotion that needs healing or medical attention.

For example, if you have a dream in which you are extremely depressed, it may be a sign that you need to seek medical help for depression. Or the Lord may be revealing that you are suffering from hopelessness and He desires to heal your heart concerning the events/context of the dream.

The Cross and Other Universal Symbols

Meanings from symbols do not emerge by coming to rational conclusions, and they are to be individually interpreted. Each symbol has to be interpreted from the dreamer's own life, feelings and background. Once again, as I have journeyed through the world of dreams, I have realized that there are *no* absolutes in interpreting symbols. In one dream, King Nebuchadnezzar was depicted as the head of a statue; in another dream he was a tree. Nothing is always, and the true interpretation belongs to the dreamer.

I have encountered familiar symbols in my ministry whose meanings seem to be universally understood. The cross is one of these; wherever I travel, a cross attached to a church, building or property represents a form of Christianity. Another popular symbol is the smiley face! While I was traveling through Japan, the language barrier became very frustrating. Many times, not only was I frustrated, the other person trying to understand my "newly developed" Japanese was also puzzled and frustrated. At the end of our conversation, to make amends, I would often draw a smiley face at the bottom of stationery, and people understood that I was conveying a form of friendly gesture—"Smile, let's be friends!" One other universal (and very popular) symbol is the McDonald's logo. When I felt hunger pains, I would begin to search for those golden arches, the symbol of *food*! When I saw them, I could always count on a Big Mac. Thank the Lord for universal food symbols in foreign countries.

No Private Interpretation of Dreams

Dream books—this one included!—containing symbolism are only to be considered reference guides *and never absolutes.* I cannot say this enough. You can be misled by limiting the voice of the Holy Spirit to a few books explaining dream language.

An excellent example of this pitfall is in interpreting the snake. Most of the time, when I dream of snakes, I interpret them as being symbolic of evil. In Scripture, however, they may represent wisdom (being wise as a serpent). Still another use of the snake is as a symbol of healing. When Israel was in sin, God allowed poisonous snakes to bite them, and many died. To bring healing, the Lord told Moses to instruct those who were bitten to look upon the brazen serpent and live. The snake actually appears in modern symbols of medicine in the staff of Asclepius, the Greek god of medicine.

From the book of Genesis, we understand that the serpent is a cursed animal. When Jesus adopted the snake as a symbol of Himself, He also took the curse of sin, sickness and death on Himself when He went to the cross:

> Just as Moses lifted up the [bronze] serpent in the desert [on a pole], so must the Son of Man be lifted up [on the cross], so that whoever believes will in Him have eternal life [after physical death, and will actually live forever].
>
> John 3:14–15 AMP

This is why healing came to the Israelites from the symbol of the snake: The serpent was the symbol of the curse. The snake (the curse) being lifted up on a pole was symbolic of Jesus becoming the curse and being lifted up. As the Israelites looked to the snake to be healed, we look to Jesus, the One who heals us from the curse. Praise the Lord forever—Jesus became the curse to ensure our being healed!

So, you see, a snake may be interpreted several different ways, which is why it is important to hear from the Holy Spirit Himself about our interpretations. If God would just give us simple and universal symbols, dreams would be somewhat easier to interpret. In reality interpretation is not that easy. All too often, we are given dreams of a complex nature. Having several dream interpretation resources ensures safe interpretation, but (Can you tell I am hammering this in?), please remember we must always use discernment when interpreting dreams! There is no single source for interpretation. Even though I myself provide a chapter on personal dream symbols, I encourage you to use it only as a guide.

Spiritual discernment is always a necessity in dream interpretation. At times, you can interpret your dreams by how you feel when you awake—were you troubled, or were you afraid or concerned in the dream? Did you feel anxious when you awoke? Note your general conclusion concerning the dream, and then ask the Lord to sharpen your discernment as you begin to study the different symbolic meanings. Even if you feel certain you know the interpretation, always pause to ask the Lord for the full, divine interpretation. Our natural instincts cannot always be trusted, whereas our divine giftings (like discernment) will lead us to the heart and thoughts of God.

Your Inner Witness

Keep in mind this one important thing as you continue to journey through the world of symbolism and dream interpretation: Every dream from God is delivered with an innate passion to search for its true meaning. It is such a strong drive that you will not be able to ignore it! That is because God's Spirit inside you will continue to speak to your "inner witness" to guide you into all truth. Though others may attempt to sway you or attempt to interpret your dream and convince you of a particular interpretation, your default button will always be your inner witness, or to what I also refer as your spiritual discernment.

This is the reason why, at times, you cannot shake off certain dreams. When that occurs, it means that the dream has great significance and has a divine premium placed on it by the Lord Himself!

As you learn more concerning symbolism and how to properly apply it to your life, you will also learn the importance of confirmation. Confirmation flows with your inner witness. It can be defined as the divine ability to hear further from God concerning your dream's meaning and spiritual significance, and it comes in many different ways: through another dream, His audible voice, visions, mental pictures and through the voices of others, such as prophets and pastors. Your inner witness is similar to covert knowledge of a dream's meaning. In other words, further knowledge and understanding confirm whether your interpretation is correct or incorrect.

Proper Responses to Your Dreams

Philippians 2:12 states that we must walk out our salvation. Dreams and visions given to us by God empower us to walk out our lives! Remember that the word *salvation* comes from the Greek word *sozo*, "to save." Daily we can walk out all that *sozo* has to offer us. Do you remember what that is? It is healing, protection, blessing, prosperity, safety, being saved and all that heaven has to offer! A proper response to *any* word from God involves *our* responding properly to that word.

As we daily walk with the Lord, it is important to keep asking for His gifts and then exercising those gifts. But allow me to be blunt—we must at some point be *accountable* to God with all that He speaks to us concerning dreams and visions. Now, let's look at some proper responses to your dreams and visions.

Wake Up and Write

One of the simplest ways to be accountable with any dream is to wake up and write! Journaling your dreams is priceless. Let's look again at Daniel's example: "In the first year of Belshazzar king of Babylon Daniel had a dream and visions of his head upon his bed: then *he wrote the dream*, and told the sum of the matters" (Daniel 7:1 KJV, emphasis mine).

Do not concern yourself over every minute detail or just *how* to write it out. There is really no right or wrong way to document dreams. It is your dream, so document it so that you can pray over it. You can draw it, put it in outline form, write a brief summary . . . do what is needed to empower *you*! Make it easier to document the dreams by placing a dream journal and a pen beside your bed before you sleep. A journal could be a simple notebook labeled "Dreams and Visions." Over the years, I have found that the easiest form of documentation is a loose-leaf binder in which pages can be inserted. As more interpretation is revealed, I can simply add more sheets and not be concerned about space. Some people log their dreams into a computer.

When waking from a dream, immediately document symbols, scenes, people, etc., and sequence. Again, documenting your feelings upon awakening can prove to be extremely important. Documenting a dream at 3:00 in the morning is difficult for some. If necessary, record only the symbols that will trigger your full recollection in the morning. If you start having long dreams and you are writing every single word, you may become frustrated and quit journaling. Journaling will take time and effort, but if you begin documenting key symbols, it will spark your memory the next morning, and you can write the full dream during waking hours.

Thus, there are several ways to document your dreams. One simple form of documentation is provided below, in which you give the dream a title and date and then list symbols with interpretations.

Dream Chart

Title of Dream		Date
Backdrop		
Symbol	Interpretation	
Interpretation		

Another way is to draw the dream, to the best of your ability. Say your dream involved airplanes flying over a mountain and trees. As you draw, other details might come to mind, such as there being two mountains rather than one. You might remember trees and flowers growing on one of the mountains, which could represent a season.

Another direction is to pick out the main character and then make all types of notes about that person. List any other important objects, people, etc., and then make notes of what significance they might have in the dream. Remember, if you are not the main subject of the dream, you are basically an observer. The dream, therefore, is not directly about you. This is a dream that is usually meant for prayer. Make notes of how you might pray, and also make notes about the person in the dream.

Some find it more convenient to use a recorder. If you are using a recorder, simply talk into the microphone (or your phone) upon awakening. The next morning replay the dream and then document all the details in your dream journal. Remember to share the feelings you are experiencing during the dream. Do not trust yourself to remember the dream in the morning, because most of the time the memory fails.

Do not forget to assign every dream a title and include the date the dream was received. Titles and dates will later prove to be important as the Lord continues to unfold His revelation.

Remain Teachable

It is *always* important to remain in a place of accountability. Any time we are moving in areas of prophetic insight, we need spiritual guidance and accountability. Spiritual oversight is especially necessary when you have dreams concerning other church members or concerning church direction. Submit dreams you feel are important to your pastors, your elders or someone in authority. Ask for prayer assistance to determine dream revelation and interpretation. The leaders may have a key that you need. Lift up your pastors and prepare your heart by praying that the Lord speak through them. A dream does not merit a proud spirit because you believe you have heard from God. Remember that your dream can originate from several sources and, in fact, may *not* be from God. Do not think that you have all of the answers or that your pastor is wrong if he or she does not move in the direction of your desire.

Treat Interpretations as You Would a Prophetic Word

Prophecy is the voice of God spoken through the mouth of anyone who will listen to Him and is willing to speak. Dreams are another aspect of God speaking. As we saw in Joel 2:28, the Lord is pouring out His Spirit upon His sons and daughters.

This includes both prophecy and dreams. Since dreams are just another way for the Lord to speak, it could be termed "prophecy while you sleep." I strongly urge you to respond to dreams and visions as you would to prophetic words by utilizing proper prophetic procedures. It is not wise to force the interpretation of a dream—nor to force a prophetic word to come to pass. Patience is necessary in your journey of understanding God's languages.

The prophetic word brings life. Ezekiel 37 describes the power of the prophetic word: When Ezekiel prophesied to dry bones, the bones began to move and come together. The bones were activated with *life* when the prophetic declaration was released. As a result, the dead bones became a vast and mighty army. When prophecy is spoken, things begin to *move* in the Spirit realm. Supernaturally, there is a divine shift in the heavenlies, and the dry areas of our lives that seem dead begin to show fruitfulness. This is one way to "wage a good warfare" with the Word of the Lord: "This charge I commit unto thee, son Timothy, according to the prophecies which went before on thee, that thou by them mightest war a good warfare" (1 Timothy 1:18 KJV).

No Contradiction of the Written Word

Dreams from the Lord never contradict what the Lord has spoken in His written Word. A dream about intimacy with someone other than one's spouse would obviously not grant permission for adultery since God's written Word expressly forbids it. God builds line upon line and precept upon precept. If a dream does not build on what God has already established, it is not from the Lord.

All godly dreams will align with His Word. The Word is the standard by which all revelation and interpretation should be measured; 2 Timothy 3:16 says, "All scripture is given by inspiration of God, and is profitable for doctrine, for reproof, for correction, for instruction in righteousness."

With the foundation laid, it is time now to look at my personal A–Z dictionary of symbolism. These symbols are taken from my own dreams and the revelation of countless others. I believe these will empower you as you interpret your dreams. But remember, the Lord desires to build *your own personal* dream vocabulary! So, again, these chapters on symbolism are only to be used as a guide. Allow the Holy Spirit to continue to speak, build and reveal your dream language.

9

A–Z Dictionary of Symbolism

*M*y intent for writing this book was to introduce you to the Master Potter in such a way that you understood how He molds us and fashions us into His divine image. He uses dreams to do just that! As you have learned, dreams and visions are the major ways God speaks to us; therefore, it is wisdom to study the symbols within our dreams and visions so that we can properly respond to His voice. While it is true, as you have also learned, that not all dreams are from God, you will find that once you understand how He speaks in symbolism, you will be better equipped to discern the source of the dream.

With that in mind, it is time to provide you with my reference list of symbol meanings. Every interpretation must be completely dependent on the Lord's directives, so remember to ask Him first concerning the meaning of the symbolism in your dreams. Always let the Holy Spirit be your filter. He alone is the final authority when interpreting your dreams and visions.

When you are searching through this list, do remember the following: (1) This list is a general guide only; (2) it is not comprehensive; (3) one must never—*never*—depend entirely on one list when attempting to interpret a dream or vision from God; and (4) *nothing is always!* As I have stated, when God is speaking we need to be listening to *Him*. My list is not divine direction; it is merely a tool—one of many tools available to help us interpret God's dream language. In the bibliography I have listed a number of fantastic references that I highly recommend studying. In addition to my own personal revelation, I drew heavily on them in forming this A–Z list.

You will notice that most of the symbols have more than one meaning, and many symbols carry positive *and* negative messages. When interpreting, keep your discerner turned on! Here is a rundown of the important questions to ask yourself when interpreting symbols:

- What were my emotions during the dream?
- Was I at peace? Was I fearful?
- Did I see colors?
- Was I a participant or was I simply an observer?

The context of every dream will determine the direction you should go with your interpretation. You will develop your own personal vocabulary of symbols, but remember that a dog to you may mean a pet, while to someone else it represents fear and terror. (This is an example of my theory that nothing is always when interpreting dreams and visions.)

My prayer for you is that you will use this list to unlock further revelation from the Holy Spirit concerning how to understand God's messages to you. I pray that you are led by the Holy Spirit and His divine wisdom as He unveils hidden mysteries and continues to speak to you in His heavenly language.

Symbols A–Z

Abandoned garage: no vehicle to get you where you need to be, hopelessness, isolation and loss of vision.

Abandoned house: barrenness and desolation, infertility.

Abandoned road: deserting God's plans for one's life, following fleshly desires, stubbornness and rebellion, works of the flesh.

Abandoned vehicle: symbolic of an unused calling, gifting or ministry; the anointing of God being dormant.

Abandonment: feeling of hopelessness, despair and rejection; the need for a natural/spiritual mother and father; feeling cursed and unwanted.

Abortion: a premature death of a deep desire, mission or a new season in your life. Sometimes represents the actual act of abortion, but most of the time not literally.

Acid: a wounded and bitter spirit, bitterness, offenses and hatred, something eating at you such as bad memories and emotions, emotional pain.

Actor: this is non-sex-specific and usually symbolizes playing some type of role or responsibility. An actor or actress also symbolizes various roles he or she played in certain movies.

Admiral: high rank, important authority figure.

Adultery: idolatry, putting other things above God, fear of betrayal, distrust, unfaithfulness.

Aging: gaining wisdom through life's circumstances, having great insight, maturity, having a place of honor among others.

Air force: the need for spiritual warfare in the heavenly realm, high level of spiritual warfare, battling and/or exposing the prince of the power of the air, the need for prayer covering.

Airplane: personal ministry, or large and/or worldwide ministry, that is flowing in speed and great power.

Airport: preparing to launch or "take off" into a new endeavor, departing an old season and entering the new, leaving and entering.

Alarm/alarm clock: being awakened to do something, a wake-up call, a call to prayer.

Alcohol: current, former or generational stronghold and addiction.

Alien/space alien: heavenly visitors—both demonic and God's angels. The dream content will determine whether the angels are good or evil.

Alligator: Leviathan, which manifests as pride (Job 3:8, 41:1; Isaiah 27:1), also described as sea monster and dragon. Big mouth, strong jaws can refer to the "jaws of death." Also implies arrogance, anger and divination through malicious lies and gossip.

Almond blossom: a new season in life and God's anointing on a ministry.

Almond tree: God watching over His Word and promises concerning our lives and ministries (Jeremiah 1:11–12).

Altar: laying down one's life for the work of the ministry, symbolic of worship and sacrifice (both godly and evil).

Ambulance: urgent situation ahead needing immediate attention and care.

Amish: the need to not conform to the world but be transformed by the renewing of the mind, separating oneself from evil influences.

Amusement park: childlike faith, fun, excitement and loving life.

Anchor: hope (Hebrews 6:19), connected, stable.

Angels: God sending specific messages, help and protection, being ministered to by the Lord.

Ankles: having little faith or beginner's faith. (See the ankle-deep waters in Ezekiel 47:3.)

Antenna: the need to listen closely and tune in to God's voice and Word, tuning in to God's frequency.

Ants: industriousness, nuisances, harmful words (bites).

Apocalypse: the end times (Revelation 13:7), perilous times.

Apple: partaking of something forbidden (Genesis 3:6). A gold apple might imply that wisdom is needed. Apples, if supported by context, symbolize the presence of God and His divine times of refreshing (Song of Solomon 2:5).

Apple tree: warning against a temptation, a husband's love (Song of Solomon 2:3).

Apron: servanthood and the need to develop the heart of a servant, the need to anoint prayer cloths and give to the sick (Acts 19:11–12).

Aquarium: exposure and shame (living in a fishbowl where everyone can see), feeling trapped, having vision but being unable to take steps into fulfillment, a ministry call of an evangelist (to be a fisher of men).

Architect: heavenly plans being drawn for breakthrough and building the Kingdom of God, plans that God has drawn concerning one's life and destiny.

Ark: God's covenant promise to protect and save during difficult times and storms of life.

Ark of the Covenant: covenant promises and His presence, the Most Holy Place, the mercy seat.

Arm: the presence of God. A right arm is symbolic of blessing; the left arm is symbolic of judgment.

Armor: God's protection for believers, the need to put on the full armor of God, spiritual warfare.

Army: the army of the Lord, a group of people coming together to defeat evil or for an intended cause, prophetic words of life needing to be spoken (the valley of dry bones).

Arrows: weapons of the enemy, lies and deceit (Jeremiah 9:8), God's children. An arrow in the back represents fear, running from needed confrontations, not advancing upon the enemy.

Ashes: deep grief, sorrow, loss, hopelessness, repentance, mourning, memories, ruin, destruction.

Aspirin: situation that needs healing and relief from physical or emotional pain.

Assassins: demonic forces with evil intent to kill, steal and destroy; terrorism.

Astrological signs: divination, witchcraft, seeking ungodly direction.

Astronaut: seeing into the unseen heavenly realm, seeing/visiting heavenly places or high levels in the Spirit realm.

Athlete: playing in the game of life, being competitive (both good and bad), striving, works-oriented.

ATM: money coming from God or others, financial breakthrough, money is "on its way"!

Attic: hidden motives, feeling "boxed in," memories, pent-up memories and emotions, high place of worship and prayer (2 Chronicles 33:17).

Attorney: intercessor, mediator, Jesus as our Mediator, someone who chooses words well or needs to, determined to accomplish a desired end result.

Automobile: an individual's anointing, life and/or personal ministry.

Autumn: end of a season, change, repentance.

Axe: a weapon for spiritual warfare and a sign of deliverance, pruning. A battle axe represents the Word of God, because the Word is a weapon against the enemy when spoken.

B

Baby: birthing, entering into something new and fresh, intimacy, new vision, dependency, helpless situations.

Baby food: the need for spiritual maturity, feeding on God's Word.

Back door: a sneak attack from the enemy, the need to close a spiritual door.

Backstage: something unseen, hidden, secretive, waiting to be revealed, someone about to come forth and be noticed by others.

Baggage: carrying around emotions/memories/pain from the past or past relationships, the need to move forward in life, finances available to move forward.

Baking: a heated situation, preparing for a particular ministry, being under fire, persecution.

Bait: feeling "hooked," addictions, warning, a lure or a trap.

Balancing: overwhelming feeling of being out of control, the need for balance and order in one's life, warning to carefully make a decision, keeping stable in the midst of a crisis.

Balding hair: shame, being uncovered, not having adequate protection or prayer.

Ball gown: preparing to dance with the King, preparing for any situation in which grace is recognized and given.

Ballroom: the need to dance and rejoice, having joy and fun.

Band-Aid: needing to cover a wound (with prayer, etc.) for healing, attempting to tackle a large problem with few or no resources.

Banker: the Lord our provider, angel, accountant, resources becoming available.

Bankrupt: emotionally and spiritually drained, a warning of some type of collapse.

Baptism: death to self, new beginning.

Bar: surrounded by negativity and evil influences.

Barbed wire: demonic assignment to hinder or stop forward progression and the fulfilling of dreams and destiny; feeling fenced in emotionally due to sharp, hurtful words from others; the pain of injustice.

Barking: warning that a predator is near, warning of the presence of an evil spirit.

Barn: stored up blessings, harvest, inheritance about to be released.

Barrenness: being unproductive or unfruitful, hopelessness, being in a wilderness season.

Basement: being "under" pressure, humility, stored-up emotional pain, wanting to hide.

Bat: witchcraft, evil, preying, darkness, unclean spirit.

Bathing/showering: cleansing, deliverance.

Bathrooms: cleansing and deliverance, a "rest room" (meaning needing to rest).

Battery: the need to "recharge," running low on energy, needed power and strength.

Battle: spiritual battle, God's desire to empower us to win.

Battleship: the Church being fully equipped for spiritual warfare, the need to prepare for war.

Bear: warning to beware of something evil, something seducing or cunning, the destroyer, danger.

Beard: age and wisdom (gray beard), an authority figure.

Beauty shop: place of being prepared and fashioned, vanity.

Beaver: busy building the Kingdom of God, too busy.

Bed: sickness, attack of a Jezebel spirit, a need to rest, covenant relationship (intimacy).

Bedroom: intimacy, something private and confidential, the need to relax and rest.

Bee: Deborah anointing, judgments (good and bad), producing sweetness (honey), sting, betrayal, evil gossip.

Belching: deliverance from an evil influence.

Bell: the announcement of something, a beckoning call, an announcement of an important event, danger.

Belly: innermost being, worldly appetite and lust.

Belt: truth, the need for the armor of God, spiritual warfare, tearing down the lies of the enemy.

Bible: using God's ultimate authority in a situation, speaking forth the Word, proclaiming the truth, the need to dig into the Word and spend time with the Lord.

Bicycle: expending effort by oneself, works of the flesh, self-righteousness, legalism, working through life's challenges alone, messenger.

Billboard: an important message and/or warning to heed. What is written on the billboard is the actual message.

Bird: Holy Spirit (dove), messenger, evil (vulture), freedom.

Birth control pills: the need to control one's own life, presence of a Jezebel spirit influencing decisions.

Birthday gifts: celebration, celebrating life, gifts and favor coming into your life, spiritual gifts.

Blood: life (life is in the blood), covenant, murder, sin, generational strongholds, curses.

Blossoms: new season, favor, coming into fruitfulness and blessing.

Blanket: the need to "cover up" something, shame, spiritual covering and/or protection.

Blindness: spiritually unable to see and/or understand, legalism, Pharisee, ignorance of God's love and desires for a person/ministry.

Blueprints: God's plans and strategies used in building one's life and ministry.

Boat: ministry; recreation and relaxation; support; if in a storm, it is a time of testing; time to step out of the boat with faith.

Bombs: explosion or power (good and bad).

Bones: the need to have structure in one's life, having a broken spirit, grief. A skeleton symbolizes spiritual death or death to vision.

Book: a lesson to be learned, the need to study, gaining revelation, student, teacher.

Bow: a weapon in war, spiritual warfare, judgment.

Box: feeling "boxed in," ungodly control, helpless, completeness.

Brass: Word of God, judgment, human tradition.

Bread: Jesus Christ (the Bread of Life), life, the need to feed on the Word of God, taking Holy Communion, sowing and reaping (casting your bread upon the water).

Break: separation, failure, fear of losing control, the need for self-control, unable to stop (addiction, gossip, etc.).

Brick: Pharaoh, Satan, slavery and bondage, effort of the self, hard work, laboring under extreme pressure.

Bride: covenant, the Bride of Christ, the Church, the need for purity.

Bridegroom: Jesus Christ.

Bridge: the need to connect, crossing over.

Bridle: needing restraint, self-control, guarding the tongue, watching over words spoken, held back from achieving deep desires, hindrances.

Broom: cleansing (sweep it out!). A broomstick represents witchcraft and possible curses.

Brother: literal brother, a close friend, a church member.

Brother-in-law: literal brother-in-law, brother in ministry, oneself, showing partiality or conflict.

Bruise: Jesus providing whatever is needed (Isaiah 53:5), spiritual warfare, affliction.

Bugs: fear, irritations, destruction.

Bull: persecution, danger, spiritual warfare (bullfight, fighting for one's life).

Bulldog: stubbornness; tenacity; strength; if personal pet, it is a "precious thing."

Bullets: words spoken with harmful intent, malicious gossip, deep wounding.

Burglar/robber/thief: Satan (John 10:10); enemy who seeks to steal, kill and destroy; invasion of one's personal life.

Buried alive: fear of death, warning of a sudden danger, overwhelming circumstances, desperately out of control.

Burning bush: an encounter with God as He reveals a divine calling or commissioning; an encouragement that one can press past personal weaknesses to be empowered by God to fulfill His Kingdom destiny on earth.

Burns: ungodly passion, being "burned" in a relationship or business, being "burned out" in ministry and needing to rest.

Bus: large ministry, large move of God, corporate ministry and anointing, being on a spiritual journey.

Butterfly: transformation and change, freedom, renewing the mind, flighty, glory, beauty.

C

Cab/taxi: temporary situations that are occurring during one's life journey, such as a temporary move, job or challenge (both physical and emotional).

Cabin: the need to separate, a time for seclusion and rest, the need for peace.

Cafeteria: making quality choices in life, servanthood.

Cage: fear of being trapped, actual entrapment, bondage, addiction, the need for the flesh to be "tamed."

Calendar: God's perfect timing for a realized promise, the need to seriously consider one's busy schedule, fitting something into the schedule, call to schedule time for prayer and time with God, call to pay attention to the season one is in, change.

Calf: idolatry, false worship, enlargement (when a calf beaks out of a stall).

Camel: endurance, long-suffering, burden bearer, servanthood, goes the distance, loyalty, strength in the desert, God's grace during a wilderness season (He will carry you!), a long journey, supernatural provision.

Camouflage/wearing fatigues: the need to remain careful and on alert, spiritual warfare, a reminder of being hidden in Christ (Colossians 3:3).

Cancer: an actual illness that needs attention; if spiritual, it could symbolize something spreading in the Body of Christ that needs immediate attention; something "eating" at you.

Candlestick: represents light, the Church, the Holy Place, the Tabernacle of God, being a light in the world (witness of Christ).

Capitol building: governmental authority, the need to pray for a specific state, country or public office.

Car: see *automobile.*

Car crash: hindering situations concerning the fulfillment of one's life, calling and ministry; a warning that prayer is needed.

Carpenter: Jesus Christ, restoration, the Lord building your life.

Carpet: the need to cover up something, shame.

Cat: witchcraft, being "bewitched," sneaky, cunning, crafty, stalker, predator, self-willed, a precious thing such as a personal pet.

Caterpillar: slow movement, "inching away in life," judgment, curses, the need for transformation.

Catholicism: religious tradition, religious legalism, doctrines of men.

Cave: running from a Jezebel spirit, needing to hide, running from an evil assignment, a place of encouragement, God's presence.

Cemetery: death of personal ambition, death of a dream or desire, putting something to rest.

Chain: bondage, oppression, slavery. A key chain possibly represents a ministry about to open up (key to a vehicle), a door being opened and/or using the keys of the Kingdom.

Chair: seat of godly authority, being seated with Christ, a seat of Satan in the hearts of men.

Chariot: spiritual warfare, victory in warfare, glory.

Chased: fear, being pursued by an evil spirit or enemy.

Cheerleader: encouragement to stay in the race/game, victory. Do not quit!

Chicken: fearful, spirit of fear, unbelief structures, watchful (a mother hen brooding over her chicks), cowardice, lack of courage, gossip, feeling like the enemy and/or life circumstances are "pecking away" at you (wearing you down).

Chief: authority figure, encouragement to pray for the Native Americans, generational curses to be broken, fierce in battle.

Children: one's life as a child, innocent, multiplication, fruitfulness, childlike faith.

Christmas tree: birthing, a new thing coming forth, joy, peace, gifts of the Spirit, traditions of men.

Cigarette: addiction, the need for deliverance, something being "rolled up."

Cinderella: living a "fairy tale" life; denial; being protected by God, our fortress; having hope for the future.

Circle (round like a ring): covenant, never-ending love of God, generational assignment and/or curses, eternity, a wilderness.

Civil war: the enemy attempting to bring division on a large scale in a nation, government, church, ministry, etc.; a "family feud."

Classroom: see *school*.

Clay: being molded by the Master Potter, the need to surrender one's will.

Climbing: moving upward, contending with anything opposing going to a higher level or promotion.

Clock: "It's time!"; exhortation to be waiting for the right time, the necessity to be on time with

God's purposes for our lives, running out of time.

Closet: the need to pray, a place to hide, darkness.

Clothes: Dirty clothes indicate a need for cleansing (pay attention to the actual piece of clothing and its color).

Clouds: God's protection and leading (Exodus 13:22), covering, hidden, mystery of God, troubling thoughts, confusion, not being clear, being in a storm.

Clown: a demonic mocking spirit, a three-ring circus situation (confusion), acting childish, the need to be serious.

Coat: spiritual covering, spiritual mantle of authority, a need to cover something up, hide.

Coffee: a wake-up time, arise, the need to become motivated.

Coffin: someone's actual death, suffocating situation, dying to self, death of a dream/vision, being in a rut.

Colors: Noting certain colors in dreams proves very valuable, as colors are a tremendous aid in interpreting dreams. Colors and numbers have both positive (godly) implications and negative (demonic) implications.

Color	Positive	Negative
Amber	Change, change of seasons.	Frustration, hopelessness, rebellion.
Black	Dusk; even in a dark dream God uses black to empower us to see into the plans of the enemy.	Extreme lack, loss, sin, death, afflictions, famine, wickedness, occult, evil, demonic realm, depression, hopelessness, a season that feels "dark" in which you are isolated.
Blue	Open heaven, revelation, divine encounter, Holy Spirit, heavenly minded, mind of Christ, wisdom, holiness.	Depression, sadness, feeling blue, anxiety.
Light blue	Immature in moving in the gifts, a student in the supernatural, peace.	Arrogance, pride, rebellion, jealousy.
Ocean blue/ dark blue	Deep calling unto deep, deep revelation.	Feeling as if drowning, hopelessness, occult.
Bronze (or brass)	Forgiveness of sins, strength.	Judgment, flesh, weakness, selfish ambition.

Color	Positive	Negative
Brown	God's love for mankind, compassion, creation of man, repentance.	Humanism, self-righteousness, works of the flesh, rebellion, dead works.
Gold	God's glory, the throne of God, value, mercy.	Selfish ambition, self-righteousness.
Gray	Divine wisdom, mature.	Having "gray" areas, compromise, unclear motives, untrustworthiness, old and dying.
Green	Life, increase, prosperity, peace.	Envy, fleshly motives, jealousy, poverty.
Orange	Power source (the sun), ability to break through darkness.	Witchcraft, danger ahead, warning, harm.
Pink	Childlike faith (pink skin of a newborn), innocence.	Flesh, being sensual and seductive, hard-hearted to the things of God.
Purple	Royalty, godly authority, rule, kingship.	Illegitimate authority, Absalom spirit.
Red	Blood of Jesus that cleanses sin and promises salvation, divine healing, protection and restoration, passion.	Anger, ungodly emotions, lust.
Scarlet	Redemption, the blood of Jesus.	Sin, idolatry (animal sacrifices).
Silver	Redemption, salvation, having great value, passed the test in the midst of the fiery trial.	Furnace of affliction, religious spirits, legalism, worthlessness.
White	Purity, righteousness, becoming the Bride of Christ, innocence.	Religious spirit, works mentality, self-righteousness.
Yellow	Courage, hope, light of God, Sun (the Son).	Fear, cowardice, shy, timid, insecure, identity crisis.

Colt: stubbornness, immaturity, bearing burdens, feeling as if you are "carrying" the work of the ministry.

Comforter: the Comforter, the Holy Spirit; a spiritual covering.

Computer: gathering information, the need to "look up."

Cooking: preparing spiritual food, a message coming forth for "feeding the sheep."

Copy machine: see *Xerox*.

Corn: season of harvest, blessing, manifestation of generational and spiritual inheritances.

Covered wagon: pioneering a new move of God.

Costume: hypocrite, attempting to cover up who one really is, deception.

Crow (raven): confusion, darkness, evil, unclean, God's covenant promise of provision (Elijah in the wilderness).

Crowing: denying Christ, cowering under peer pressure, persecution, fear of man.

Crown: royalty; spiritual inheritance; a symbol of honor, reward and victory.

Crystal ball: witchcraft, divination, wanting answers too quickly and not waiting on God's direction.

D

Dam: blockage, stopping a move of the Spirit, hindrances in life/ministry, a major flow of the Spirit.

Dancing: worship, idolatry, freedom, freedom of expression, seduction.

Daughter: actual daughter, daughter in the Spirit, a gift.

Death: warning of potential actual death, a demonic assignment, death of vision, hopelessness, a time of separation.

Deer: graceful, swift, spiritual hunger, being sure-footed.

Demon: evil spirit, needed prayer to overcome the plans of the enemy.

Dentist: watching over what comes out of the mouth, watching our words, needing spiritual mentoring concerning the Word of God, needing someone to help with wisdom.

Desert: a type of wilderness, isolation, testing, barrenness, thirsting for God.

Diamond: hard-heartedness, covenant promises (especially if a diamond ring), beauty, strength.

Dinosaur: outdated, the need for a situation or a person to disappear.

Diving: headed into danger, headstrong, going deep in the Spirit.

Doctor: Jesus Christ, the great physician (Jeremiah 8:22); the need to literally visit a doctor.

Dog: something precious, such as a personal pet; obedience; loyalty; a barking dog might be a warning; an unbeliever or religious hypocrite.

Dominoes: unfortunate events that are uncontrollable.

Donkey: stubbornness, God speaking through an unlikely source.

Door: Christ, opening, a new beginning, breakthrough. A closed door could represent hindrances to moving forward.

Dove: Holy Spirit, God resting on us, gentleness.

Dragon: the spirit of Leviathan, the Antichrist and his evil forces.

Dreaming within a dream: These dreams reveal something futuristic that involves destiny. Pay close attention to them!

Dripping faucet: gossip, release of revelation at a slow pace, disagreements and arguments, constant criticism that wears one down.

Driving: The one driving is the one in control.

Driving backward: losing progress, backsliding.

Driving fast: being in a hurry, moving too fast.

Driving slowly: a need to speed up, the need to be cautious.

Drowning: overwhelmed, hopelessness, deep sorrow and depression, wanting to die, alert from the Holy Spirit that prayer and counsel are needed.

Drugs: codependent relationships, sorcery, witchcraft, medicine, healing.

Dynamite: an explosion, danger coming, an emotional explosion.

E

Eagle: seer, prophet (true or false), watchman on the wall, intercessor, swiftness, ability to soar.

Ear: the ability to hear what God is speaking, remaining attentive.

Earthquake: upheaval, a separation, shock, disaster, rebellion (spirit of Korah), God's judgment and the calling for repentance, a spiritual shaking.

Eating: being fed spiritually or naturally, partaking, covenant relationship.

Egg: a time to wait and allow incubation.

Egypt: bondage, slavery, sinful nature.

Elementary school: learning the basics, going back to foundations, the need to mature.

Elephant: spirit of Behemoth, invincible, thick-skinned, sin not dealt with that can no longer remain hidden, the need to remember.

Elevator: going up a level; promotion; extending into the heavenlies for revelation; if going down, demotion.

Elves: messengers and helpers (both good and evil).

Emotions: Emotions revealed in dreams are mostly literal; signal to depend completely on the Lord rather than "feelings."

Employer: actual employer, authority figure, Father God, leadership (both good and bad).

Ex-spouse or -lover: holding on to the past, old emotions that need healing.

Exercise: the need for strength, increasing in strength and power, the need to exercise restraint and/or godly character.

Eyes: ability to see (a seer anointing), seeing what is hidden, understanding and revelation, passion, luring, seduction, the need to open one's eyes.

F

Face: identity, character, countenance, expression, image.

Fainting: the need for nourishment or spiritual strength, fear, startling news.

Fairy: a familiar, demonic spirit that is hovering over a particular person or ministry; fantasy.

Falling: fear of losing control, backsliding (falling into sin), the loss of support.

Falling and immediately waking: This is an example of a "wake-up" dream, a dream to awaken the dreamer to something very important.

Fame: favor (both in the natural and spiritual realms).

Fangs: vicious gossip, words that cut deep, lies, jealousy.

Farmer: an apostle who "plants" churches, a spiritual leader who sows seeds into believers' lives, the principle of sowing and reaping.

Father: Father God, actual father (natural or spiritual), authority figure.

Father-in-law: the Law, legalism, problem with authority figure, contention, actual natural father-in-law.

Feathers: covering, protection, Holy Spirit intervention and divine protection, angelic intervention.

Feet: authority (foot on neck of enemy), taking ground, walking away from or toward something, kicking (rebellion).

Fence: limitations, boundaries, protection, obstacles to overcome, strongholds.

Ferris wheel: "going around the mountain again," doing the same thing over and over and not realizing desired results.

Fig: Israel as a nation, sweetness, love.

Fig leaves: attempting to hide sin, unfruitfulness, rebellion, shame.

Fig tree: the need to deal with an area in life that is not fruitful.

Finger: instruction, direction and/ or deliverance (finger of God); pointing; spiritual discernment.

Fire: the presence of God, purification, holiness, testing, (fiery) trial, passion.

Fire extinguisher: the need to extinguish something harmful, such as trouble, gossip, disagreements and division.

Fish: evangelism, souls, humanity, sport, recreation.

Fishhook: being caught, hooked and/or found out.

Fistfight: spiritual warfare, the need to tear down structures of unbelief that rob faith, personal offense toward someone that needs resolving, needing vindication.

Flag: a specific nation or group that may need prayer and intercession, a missionary call to a particular nation.

Fleece: confirmation, testing God, gaining approval.

Flies: evil spirits; Beelzebub, the "lord of flies."

Floating: the ability to rest in the midst of a storm, empowerment of God's grace to rise above problems, peace.

Flood: being overwhelmed, a flood of demonic opposition that needs God's intervention, judgment of sin, a spiritual breakthrough, a major move of God.

Floor: foundation; feeling "walked on"; being on the floor represents humility and/or helplessness; the ground floor of a new business, building or ministry; a beginning point.

Flowers: glory, beauty, special occasions, romance, blossoming.

Flushing toilet: the need for cleansing and deliverance, the need to rid oneself of something.

Flying: making fast progress in the Spirit, unhindered, God calling you to a higher level in the Spirit, unrestrained, overcoming life's challenges, freedom.

Food: the need for spiritual nourishment, eating from good or bad sources.

Foreigner: alien, demonic, not of God, unbeliever, sin, unclean.

Forest: a place of isolation, the need to "come out of the woods," inability to see clearly (cannot see the forest for the trees), loss of direction in life.

Fortress: God, our fortress; stronghold (demonic or godly); God's protection.

Fountain: a time of refreshing, Jesus Christ.

Fox: cunning, sly, seductive.

Friend: oneself; seeing in your friend what is also in your own life; a brother or sister in Christ. The dream can also be about your actual friend and what is going on in his/her own life.

Frog: demon, demonic activity, witchcraft, unclean spirits, generational curse.

Fruit: blessings of God.

Funeral: death to a dream, despair over a situation that seems lost or hopeless.

G

Games: experiencing and living out the everyday game of life.

Gangsters: a grouping of specific demons, demonic structures, territorial strongholds.

Garbage: needing to discard something, lies and deceit, worthlessness, having no value.

Garden/gardening: good soil, fruitfulness, spiritual and natural growth, fertility, sowing and reaping.

Gasoline: adding fuel to the fire (both good and bad), the need to "tank up," prayer being the fuel that propels one's life and ministry.

Gate: entrance, opening into a new place or opportunity, enlargement, power and authority, an entrance for angelic activity (both good and bad).

Gavel: judgment, the price has been paid at the cross, declaration that "It is finished!", the need to settle a dispute or argument.

General: having a high rank in the military or ministry, chief (good or evil).

Giant: a territorial stronghold or powerful demon, a very challenging situation in which you feel ill-equipped, an overwhelming demonic attack or situation.

Gifts: spiritual gifting, God's grace and love, rewards.

Glass: fragile, frail, ability to become easily broken, transparency, being able to "see through" a situation or someone's motives.

Glasses/contact lenses: the need to see more clearly, adjusting one's vision.

Goat: carnality, Satan, accuser of the brethren, demonic activity, stubbornness, occult, the unsaved, being a "scapegoat."

God: literally the Father speaking to us in our dreams. Our heavenly Father is often symbolized by our natural, earthly father.

Gold: the glory of God, wisdom, truth, wealth and prosperity.

Golden calf: idolatry.

Golf: a project in which you must move slowly and carefully, having several specific tools for the challenges ahead, a project that involves taking one day at a time.

Grandchildren: generational blessing, generational curse, actual grandchild, legacy.

Grandparent: generational blessing or curse, wisdom, actual grandparent.

Grapes: Promised Land, fruitfulness, fruit of the Spirit.

Grass: the flesh, dead works. Green grass represents God's blessings and "green pastures."

Grasshopper: devouring evil spirits, curses, loss, destruction.

Grave: burying an issue; letting go and laying something to rest; can literally represent death.

Gray hair: wisdom, maturity.

Grim reaper: premature death assignments that need to be broken, death to vision and/or dreams.

Groceries/grocery bag: the need for spiritual nourishment, words being spoken.

Guards: angels; God, our fortress; His divine protection.

Gun: gossip, hurtful words, spiritual warfare.

Gypsy: the curse of Cain, remaining a vagabond, one who never settles down, uncommitted, chronic dissatisfaction.

H

Hair: covering (both natural and spiritual). Lack of hair or hair loss represents shame.

Haircut: the need for something to be cut off, such as a bad habit or codependent relationship.

Hallway of doors: many opportunities opening up, many choices to be made.

Hallway of mirrors: a time for introspection, a season of vulnerability, eyes opened to see into supernatural dimensions, exposing of extreme frailty.

Hammer: the Word of God, God "hammering" His Word through repetition.

Hand: blessing, judgments, spiritual warfare, works (good or evil), agreement.

Handcuffs: bondage, restriction of progress, inability to move forward.

Harlot: seducing spirits, fornication, snare.

Hat: a symbol of headship, authority, covering.

Hawk: unclean spirit.

Head: authority figure, headship, head knowledge, legalism, the mind.

Heart: emotions, desires, hidden motives.

Helmet: salvation, the need to renew the mind, the need to put on the armor of God.

Hemorrhage: backsliding, losing strength.

Hen: a pastor who protects the flock, one who gathers.

High school: moving to a higher level of understanding and revelation.

Hills: loftiness, pride, going higher, overcoming challenges in life.

Hissing: harassing and condemning demonic spirit, intimidation, fright.

Homeless person: evil spirits searching for a permanent home in which to dwell.

Honey: sweetness, busy as a bee, the anointing of Deborah.

Horn: power, strength, spiritual warfare, prophetic voice.

Horse: power and strength, spiritual warfare, moving quickly through a spiritual battle, the ability to see in the Spirit at a new level (running with the horses).

Hospital: the need for healing, a type of healing ministry, Jesus (the Healer), the Church.

Hotel: temporary meeting place, transition.

House: one's literal house, dwelling place for Holy Spirit; see chapter 6 for more details about houses.

Hurricane: trouble coming, be on guard, a spiritual attack, destruction.

I

Ice: danger (icy roads, sidewalks, etc.), the need to pray into a situation (putting ice on a broken bone or wound), unfriendliness (cold as ice).

Iceberg: Potential danger ahead!

ICU: intensive care needed.

Incense: prayers of the saints, being acceptable to God.

Incest: the perversion of a family member attempting to influence one's life, spirit of perversion, unclean spirit.

Indians: literally a call to pray for the Native Americans, possible generational strongholds.

Injury: physical or emotional wounding.

Interior decorator: the need to put your household in spiritual order. A literal interior decorator appearing in a dream represents putting things in order concerning wills, finances, etc.

Invitation: Holy Spirit inviting you to come up higher, an invitation to a divine encounter.

Iron: strength, power, stubbornness, strictness, spiritual strongholds, subduing the enemy, legalism.

Iron bars: prison, strongholds, something holding you captive so that you are unable to achieve your destiny.

Island: isolation, loneliness, seclusion.

Israel: a need to understand Hebraic roots, a call to pray for the salvation of the Jews, the need for peace, God's children.

J

Jacket: covering, protection.

Jail: feeling imprisoned, bondage, the need for deliverance.

Jail keeper: Satan, oppressor, being oppressed.

Jawbone: being empowered with supernatural strength, victorious warfare.

Jaws: trapped by the jaws of death, Leviathan (Satan).

Jesus: His invitation to salvation and all that He died to give;

healing, deliverance, protection, provision, etc.

Jewels: the people of God, heaven's riches and rewards.

Juggling: having too many irons in the fire, overactivity, doing too much at once.

Junkyard: the need to discard worthless emotions and thoughts.

Jury: someone passing judgment (good and bad), fear of being misunderstood.

K

Karate: being highly skilled in spiritual warfare.

Keyhole: the need for the right key to unlock revelation needed for a specific situation.

Keys: unlocking of doors and opportunities for forward progress, keys of the Kingdom, ability to bind and loose, victory over the enemies of God.

Kidnapped/Kidnapper: taken somewhere against one's will, an evil spirit that is attempting to take you captive.

King: Jesus Christ, supreme authority.

Kissing: intimacy, betrayal (Judas in the Garden), friendship, agreement, seduction.

Kitchen: nourishing others, a warm place in the heart.

KKK: racism, prejudice, hatred, violence, injustice.

Knees: "knee-ology," being on our knees in prayer, surrender, worship.

Knife: weapon of spiritual warfare to "cut" down the enemy.

Knocking: Jesus Christ asking entrance into our lives, something or someone attempting to enter our lives.

L

Labor: new birthing of ministry, business and/or vision; painful transition.

Ladder: different levels (as one climbs a ladder), change in spiritual position determined by either going up or down the ladder, connecting heaven to earth as one prays.

Lamb: Christ (the Lamb of God), humility, sacrifice, innocent.

Lamp: revelation, the Word of God.

Land: spiritual inheritance, promises of God.

Lawn mower: maintaining a sinless lifestyle.

Laundry: feeling as if you have been "hung out to dry," dirty laundry, letting things "air," secrets of the heart exposed.

La-Z-Boy recliner: needing to rest in God, not being watchful, lazy.

Lead (metal): heavy weight, burden, ungodly yoke, wickedness, sin, fool, foolishness.

Leaking: emotionally and physically draining situations, irritations.

Leash: limitations, bondage, someone/something restricting you from accomplishing your desires.

Leaven: hypocrisy, sin, legalism, false belief systems, doctrines of men.

Legs: taking dominion and authority, strength and grace needed to walk a holy lifestyle.

Leopard: swiftness, unexpected ambush of the enemy.

Leprosy: unclean, rejection, sin, isolation.

Letter: an important message coming.

Leviathan: a large demonic spirit or stronghold (Job 41:1), pride and arrogance. Only the Lord's power can defeat this stronghold.

Library: a hunger to know God's perfect will, the need to study to show yourself approved.

Light bulb: the need for revelation, revelation being "turned on," creative ideas coming.

Lightning: seeing the throne of God, strength and supernatural power, God's voice.

Limping: powerlessness, shame, stolen inheritance, wrestling with God, experiencing humility, can only operate in the power of the Holy Spirit and not in one's own strength.

Lion: Jesus Christ, king, royalty, nobility, courage, boldness, strength, power.

Lions' den: place of testing, a demonic plot to destroy.

Lips: the need to watch over words being spoken, spoken falsehoods, unclean speech, needed cleansing.

Liver: spiritual discernment.

Lizard: Leviathan spirit, quickness, unclean spirit, hidden.

Lock: bondage, hindrance, needing wisdom to unlock a situation.

Locusts: a swarm of devouring spirits on the attack.

Lottery: sudden financial gain.

Love: God's love, God's character, fruit of the Spirit.

Luggage: carrying baggage from the past, be prepared to move on.

M

Maggot: wicked person or spirit, death and destruction, defeat, hopelessness, "rotten attitude."

Magic/Magician: sorcery, witchcraft, a Jezebel spirit, deception, fraud, hypocrite, imposter.

Magnifying glass: getting a closer look, look further, careful examination.

Mail/Letter: important message being written, God writing on the tablet of our hearts.

Mailbox: an important and possibly prophetic message being delivered.

Mailman: prophet, messenger.

Makeup: covering of one's flaws, faults, shame.

Manager: the Lord who manages our lives, needed management.

Manna: Bread of Life, supernatural nourishment and provision from God, angels on assignment with provision from God.

Mantle: authority, spiritual office and position.

Map: direction for one's life, God's instructions for a successful journey, a literal place.

Marching: the army of God possessing the Kingdom, an army (good or bad) moving forward with intent.

Mask: disguise, double standards, imposter, untrustworthiness, deceiving spirits at work.

Measuring stick: the need to measure up, performance orientation.

Meat: strong teaching of the Word, the need for spiritual nourishment.

Mechanic: a person who empowers you in fulfilling your destiny, minister, counselor, pastor.

Medical examination: the need for introspection, spiritually and/or emotionally; a warning from the Lord to pay close attention to your spiritual condition.

Medicine: God speaking into a literal issue with a remedy for healing, something needed that offers an important solution.

Menu: the importance of making proper choices in life.

Mercy seat: God showing mercy, the Most Holy Place, the glory of God, Jesus Christ.

Microphone: having a voice that affects many people.

Microscope: the need to take a closer look at one's life or relationship with God.

Mildew: see *mold.*

Military clothing: prepare for battle, a call to war.

Milk: the Word of God, the need to establish and/or adhere to foundational truths.

Minefield: something hidden and concealed, danger, obstacles to forward movement, traps of the enemy.

Mining: digging for God's hidden truths (revelation), finding diamonds in the rough.

Minister: see *pastor.*

Mirror: the need for self-evaluation, seeing yourself the way you truly are, looking back, reflecting on situations.

Miscarriage: an actual event, termination of a project or dream, loss of ministry or calling in the beginning stages.

Missiles: a great bombardment from the enemy, extremely effective prayer and intercession against the enemy.

Mockingbird: a mocking voice, the accuser of the brethren, demonic voices, familiar spirits.

Mold: curses, sickness and disease, rottenness.

Money: financial provision, blessing, power, Mammon (in negative sense, idolatry).

Monkey: oppressive spirit, spirit of heaviness, addiction.

Monster: demonic oppressor with a purpose to cause fear, intimidation and defeat.

Moon: light in the midst of darkness, end of a particular season.

Mop: the need to clean up your life and spiritual walk with God, cleaning up after others, servanthood, humility.

Motel: someone in transition.

Moth: destructive behavior, evil spirits, a type of spirit or behavior that "eats away" at our identities and/or breakthroughs.

Mother: actual person, El Shaddai, the Church.

Mother-in-law: actual person, law, tradition, nosy, gossip.

Motorcycle: small but fast-moving ministry, efficiency, exhilarating freedom, showing off.

Mountains: kingdoms, dignity, problems to be overcome by faith and declarations, places of revelation and the presence of God.

Mouse/Mice: curse, devourer, timidity, hiding, unclean choices.

Mouth: speaking both good and evil, life's power in the words spoken.

Movie: used in dreams to show something literal. Pay attention to specific places, names, titles, etc.

Moving van: relocation, transition.

Murder: jealousy, envy, Jezebel spirit.

Mustard seed: small faith getting huge results.

Mute: deaf and dumb spirit, unable to speak up when needed or speak for self. This spirit is connected with those having seizures and imbalance issues.

Muzzle: unable or forbidden to speak, not having a voice.

N

Nail (iron): making something permanent, fixed and stable; established; security.

Nail polish: preparing for spiritual warfare, covering up so others cannot see, hiding the truth, shame.

Naked: everything being exposed, uncovered, shamefulness, vulnerability/fear of being vulnerable, pure.

Names: Research the names revealed during dreams to find their meanings, and then use the revelation to pray accordingly.

Nazi: racism, murder, ungodly authority, rebellion.

Neck: inflexible (stiff-necked), rebellious, victory (putting our feet on the necks of our enemies).

Necklace: bondage, a yoke around the neck.

Needle: addictions, seductions.

Needle, eye of: laying down our lives, ridding ourselves of every hindrance as we pursue divine destiny.

Neighbor: the family of God, a literal calling to pray for your neighbor, praying for someone very close to you.

Nest: one's home, dwelling place, the need to settle in and trust God (a nest is not the secure place; only God is).

Net: to catch (both fish and men), entrapment.

New year: new start, starting over, being offered a new opportunity.

Newspaper: prophetic declarations, written godly decrees, spreading the word (good or bad).

Nose: spiritual discernment, someone who is snoopy and "nosy," the need to mind your own business, breath.

Nudity: shame, guilt, vulnerability, uncovered, flesh, not putting on the armor of God, self-righteousness, feeling exposed, temptation, lust.

Numbers: Numbers have biblical significance, so a list of scriptural symbolism of numbers follows. A number is usually relevant to the discernment and understanding of each dreamer; as a rule, however, the numbers should be interpreted literally. Just as in the case of colors, numbers can have either a positive or negative interpretation, depending on how the dreamer determines the context of the dream. (For a deeper explanation of the importance of numbers, see chapter 7.)

Number	Positive	Negative
1	God, submitted to God, first in order and importance.	Isolation, loner, self, independence.
2	Unity, double portion, discernment.	Disunity, division, lack.
3	Trinity, three-fold cord, divine witness, Resurrection.	False doctrine, religious tradition, doctrines of man.
4	God's creation, creative abilities.	Inability to dream with God, blocked creativity, desolation, hopelessness, depression.
5	Five-fold ministry, servant-hood, God's grace, humility.	Works of the flesh, bondage, addictions, self-righteousness, pride.
6	Man created in the image of God, harmony.	The Beast (666), flesh, carnality, idolatry, rebellion.
7	Completion, perfection, divine rest, covenant, fulfilled promises.	Striving, works of the flesh, hopelessness, lack.
8	New beginnings, sanctification, circumcision, death to self.	Conformed to the world, rebellion.
9	Fruitfulness, harvest, increase, works of the Holy Spirit.	Works of the flesh, lack, loss.
10	Divine measurement, tithe.	Fiery trials, tests, times of temptation, generational curses, lack.
11	Transition, the end of a season, entering a new season.	Hindrances, obstacles, heavy weights, lawlessness, rebellion.
12	God's government, unity.	Rebellion, division, stubbornness.
13	Governmental authority, unity.	Disorder, lawlessness, dictator, control.
14	Double-portion anointing, reproduction.	Bondage, lack, addiction, barren.
15	Grace, freedom, atonement for sin.	Sinfulness, bondage, self-righteousness, pride, arrogance, rebellion.
40	Divine protection, guidance, miracles.	Wilderness, testing, rebellion, doubt and unbelief.

Nurse: a helper, someone empowering a healthy lifestyle or relationship with Christ.

Nursing/Breast-feeding: being fed directly from the Lord, feeding a godly or ungodly desire.

O

Oak: solidarity, stability, strength, people of God.

Ocean: large groups of people, God's deep truths.

Occult: witchcraft, a Jezebel spirit, may mean literal curses and spells that need to be broken.

Office: a place where authoritative decisions are made and details are given for projects.

Office building/High-rise: large-scale ministry, a supernatural ministry that is at high levels in the Spirit realm.

Oil: the anointing, the Holy Spirit, Jesus Christ (the Anointed One), medicine, joy.

Ointment: healing balm, soothing for wounds, inner healing.

Old: an old way, old patterns of behavior and/or lifestyle.

Old man: wisdom, carnality (see *ex-spouse or -lover*).

Olive branch: needing peace.

Olympics: competition (good or bad), achieving good works, the need for strength and endurance.

Onions: uncontrollable crying and sadness, grief, mourning, depression, hopelessness, the need to express pent-up emotions.

Orphan: emotional, physical or spiritual abandonment; hopelessness; outcast; rejection; serving God with religious works rather than through sonship.

Ostrich: head in the sand, denial, unaware of the needs of others, self-centered.

Ouija board: inviting demonic spirits into your life, being controlled by familiar spirits, a dangerous open door.

Oven: passion, fervency, the heart of the matter, incubating new ideas.

Owl: wisdom, witchcraft, evil, evil watchman, the ability to see in the midst of darkness.

Ox: a heavy yoke, heavy labor, strength, sacrifice.

P

Pain: literal physical or emotional pain that one is experiencing, the need for healing, a reminder of the pain Jesus suffered for our redemption so that we can receive divine healing (by His stripes we are healed).

Paint: the need to cover something up, covering up the past, shame, control, fear of rejection, applying the blood of Jesus to sin (stain).

Painter/Painting a picture: When drawing or painting a picture in a dream, pay attention to the picture itself as the revelation of a specific message to the dreamer.

Palm reading: opening your life to ungodly direction, occult, witchcraft, familiar spirits.

Panther: approaching danger, the influence of demonic realm approaching.

Paparazzi: someone of great influence coming into your life, possible success and fame coming your way, may reveal pride and presumption.

Parachute: the need to bail out of a situation or harmful relationship, having a safe landing after a threatening situation, God's promise of safety and protection after crisis.

Parade: celebration of an important event, having achieved a great victory and success.

Paralyzed: fear, being held against your will, helpless situations, enemy attempting to cripple your forward movement.

Paramedic: urgent attention needed for health or a certain situation.

Parent: actual parent in the dream, authority figure (both natural and spiritual), Father God.

Parrot: mocking spirit, something that imitates and mimics, unoriginal, malicious gossip, someone who repeats what has been heard, untrustworthiness.

Passenger: agreement with God (the one in control of your life), agreement with a partner in ministry or a move of the Holy Spirit.

Passport: a ministry call to the nations, identity in Christ.

Pastor: someone who represents God, a message from God, religion.

Path: God's direction for your life, decisions made along life's journey, the need to remain aligned with His will.

Peacock: pride, showing off, making a spectacle of oneself, narcissistic, idolatry.

Pearl: seeking the presence of God, seeking something valuable, paying a great price.

Pen/Pencil: writing, something in the written Word, a gifted scribe and/or communicator, tongue, speaking words of life and death, covenant agreements, vision, record, gossip.

Penny: extreme poverty, mindsets concerning God's desire to bless His children, giving out of a personal need (the widow's mite).

Perfume: sweet fragrance unto God, fragrance of the Holy Spirit.

Pharaoh: Satan, pride, hard-heartedness, ungodly authority, hard taskmaster, bondage, slavery.

Phone/Phone call: someone bringing you a message, God's voice, news.

Pig: uncleanness, religious spirit, hypocrite, partaking of forbidden things.

Pilot: navigating a move of God at high levels of revelation and spiritual authority, moving quickly.

Pioneers: moving into a new dimension of the Spirit, trailblazers, faithful and determined leadership.

Pirate: a robbing spirit, needing to bind the strongman.

Pit: trap, snare, a plan of destruction by those close to you (Joseph thrown in the pit by his brothers).

Pit bull: tenacity, will not give up or let go of an assignment, determined and fixed, seeks to devour others through ungodly conversations.

Plants: family tree, the need for nourishment, reaping what has been sown.

Plate: the need to take a close look at one's schedule and daily responsibilities, too much on your plate, religious works.

Play: enjoying one's life, the need to have some fun, physical or spiritual competition (good and bad).

Playing a game: a real-life situation, playing the game of life, making certain choices.

Plow: hard labor, breaking ground for a new work, preparation for the heart to receive the seeds (truths) of God.

Plumb line: lining up with God's truth, measuring.

Poison: false doctrine, lies and deceit, harmful words that have been spoken against you.

Police: the need for protection, an urgent situation that needs attention, spiritual and/or natural authority.

Pond/Pool: gathering together for fellowship and refreshing, places of baptism, receiving a new life, fresh start.

Porch: ability to be seen, vulnerability, exposure (good and bad), a time of waiting before entering a door that needs opening.

Porcupine: sharp words spoken against us, needles (addictions), pain.

Postage stamp: message that is being delivered that has a seal of authority, authorization, empowerment.

Postman: see *mailman.*

Pottery: Master Potter molding and shaping, fragility, frailty, the flesh.

Pregnancy: expectancy, the promises of God being fulfilled, a prophetic word, conceiving an idea and waiting for its manifestation.

Pressure cooker: stress, being under too much pressure, potential breakdown and emotional explosion ahead.

Prince: Jesus, the Prince of Peace; a principality; Satan; the prince of the air.

Principal: an authority figure, a demonic principality or territorial stronghold.

Prison: bondage, oppression, hopelessness, demonic strongholds.

Prophet: God's voice being spoken to you. If there is speaking in the dream, pay attention!

Prostitute: idolatry, unfaithfulness, seductions, forbidden.

Pulpit: pulling people from the pit, a calling to teach or preach.

Pumpkin: witchcraft, curses, evil deeds, demonic activity, the need to give thanks (Thanksgiving season).

Puppet: being controlled by a demonic force or evil influence, helplessness.

Purse: personal identity, wealth, finances, treasure, valuables.

Pyramid: Pharaoh, hard labor, witchcraft, occult, Egypt, the wilderness.

Python: large demonic stronghold that crushes and opposes breakthrough; stopping short of entering into enlargement; co-labors with Jezebel to steal inheritance and increase; divination; witchcraft; more information under *snakes.*

Q

Q-tip: unable to hear properly, the Word of God being "twisted" as you hear, deception, the need to clean out one's ears to hear God's voice more clearly.

Quail: God's provision during a wilderness or dry season.

Quarterback: feeling great pressure, targeted by the enemy, the need to remain steadfast and lead when under great pressure from others and demonic assignments, taking the lead and not giving a place to the devil.

Queen: could refer to a literal queen, but may also represent "the queen of heaven," an evil form of idolatry and ungodly worship; someone with great influence; the head of a nation.

Question mark: God is asking you a question—pay attention to the content of the dream and pray for a godly response; questioning your own heart; questioning other people's motives; needing direction and counsel from God and/or others.

Quicksand: the inability to stand during adversity, spiritual fortitude needed, a dangerous place or situation, the need to reach out for help, feeling as if something is "going down the tubes."

R

Rabbit: multiplication, fast growth, fertility, hopping from one project to another without completion.

Raccoon: bandit, masked, untrustworthy, mischievous, deception.

Race: finishing the race, running the race of life, strength, endurance, training, competitive spirit (both good and bad).

Radio: the need to tune in, communication in prayer, a loudmouth who is continually speaking out and expressing an opinion (both positive and negative).

Raft: drifting, having no plan for the future, without purpose and destiny, being rescued from something that was sinking.

Railroad track: confirmation that you are "on track" with God and His path for your life; God confirming that you are hearing His directives correctly; if negative, you are on the wrong track and/or not tracking properly with God.

Rain: blessings, life, revival, fruitfulness, growth, refreshing, hope, breakthrough, Holy Spirit, Word of God.

Rainbow: God's covenant promises, the need for agreement.

Rape: feeling out of control by something forced upon you, trauma.

Rapist: a demonic attack in which something is stolen from you and you feel as if you have no recourse; the demonic forcing something on you, such as disease, depression, generational curses and hopelessness; being violated; a boundary being crossed by someone with evil intent.

Rapture: Christ's second coming, a call to pray for the lost.

Rat: immorality, lack of integrity, untrustworthiness, uncleanness, devourer, wickedness, hidden motives, occult.

Raven: see *crow*.

Razor: sharp and painful words, lies.

Rearview mirror: living or focusing too much on the past, backsliding, not moving forward quickly enough, hindrances, memories of the past.

Red tape: demonic strongholds hindering the progress of building plans, breakthroughs or any needed revelation; feeling as if you must dot every *i* and cross every *t* to be approved; religious performance; legalism.

Refrigerator: hidden issues, cold-heartedness, storing up spiritually (getting in the Word), waiting for the release at the right time.

Rest: a literal need to rest, rest in God, being still before the Lord, laziness, not accomplishing your godly assignment.

Restaurant: choices made concerning your spiritual food, the need to be at the right place to be properly fed (spiritually).

Ring: God's favor on your life, His never-ending covenant, marriage to Jesus as His Bride, covenant in marriage, unity.

River: being in the flow of the Spirit, God's blessings coming forth, expectations of a breakthrough.

Roach: unclean spirit, disease, infestation, hidden sin.

Road signs: In the dream, follow the message on the sign: "Stop," "Slow," etc.; the need to pay attention to God's directives.

Robe: righteousness, rich garments, covering, mantle. (Pay attention to colors, as they will give more detail to the robe's meaning.)

Rock: Jesus Christ, solid foundation, apostle Peter and particular aspects of his ministry.

Rocket: quick start and great speed, ability to soar high in God, being launched, accelerating at a new level, jumping into something too quickly without gathering proper information or having adequate resources.

Roller coaster: emotionally unstable, moving up and down, shifting in and out of seasons, the need for activating faith, a thrilling and exhilarating situation or challenge.

Roof: place of prayer, time of meditation and prayer, God's protection during storms and life's challenges.

Rooster: being awakened, wake-up call, denial of Jesus, denial, warning of betrayal or one's potential to betray.

Rope: the need for unity, binding together, covenant, bondage.

Rose: Jesus, the rose of Sharon (Song of Songs 2:1); beauty; fragrance.

Rotten fruit: lack of fruitfulness; making wrong choices; insufficiency; due to bad fruit in one's life, there might be an inability to become fruitful and trusted.

Rowing: laboring alone in the Spirit, working things out, travail, self-effort, works of the flesh, legalism.

Rubbing: God anointing you for a specific assignment, a person opposing you and "rubbing" you the wrong way.

Rug: covering something up (good or bad), shame, guilt, the need to "soften up."

Running: competitive spirit (good or bad), attempting to move faster, attempting to catch up, winning the race.

Rust: old dreams, tarnished wishes, earthly riches, hopelessness, insufficiency, the need for cleansing.

S

Sackcloth: the need to fast and pray, mourning, extreme grief, repentance.

Sacrifice: laying down one's life, giving up something important.

Safe: hiding money and hoarding, God storing up finances in heaven and preparing to release them, God as our fortress providing safety and protection, secured life and finances.

Sails: the breath of God, being completely empowered by the Spirit.

Salmon: feeling as if you are continually swimming upstream and going against the flow, an uphill battle, independent spirit, determined to accomplish destiny regardless of resistance.

Salt: being the "salt of the earth," healing waters (saltwater).

Sandals: taking dominion in the name of Jesus, spreading the Good News as Jesus did while on earth.

Satan: Rebuke him if he is revealed in a dream. If he speaks, break the power of his words and decree what God says concerning the words and ungodly motives revealed.

Scab: a wound is healing, do not be "picky," learn to be satisfied and patient with God's plans and timing for your life.

Scar: the nail-scarred hand of Jesus and the price He paid on the cross for our healing and deliverance, past emotional pain, trauma, wounds, the need to shift into faith.

Scepter: being allowed to approach the throne of God, grace, mercy, favor, authority, sovereignty.

School: a season of training, an actual time in one's life while in school (make note of specific events that occurred in real life in case healing is needed), teaching, training, a teaching anointing.

Scissors: the need to cut something or someone off and away from your life, pruning, a spirit of Delilah that seduces and leads us astray.

Scorpion: stung from the backside, betrayal, "didn't see it coming," blindsided, evil, demonic activity, sinful nature.

Scroll: a written decree or command issued from God and sometimes delivered through angels, commissioning from God.

Sea: a multitude of people, nations, the need to cross over.

Sea monster: see *Leviathan*.

Seat: being "seated" with Christ in heavenly places, rulership, authority, the mercy seat.

Seat belt: the need to "stay put," the need for protection, God's divine protection for every situation.

Secretary: one who gathers information; helper; assistants in dreams may represent angels.

Security guard: God, our fortress; an angel; the need for protection.

Seed: the Word of God, being pregnant with vision and/or ministry, an investment that needs attention and tending, the need to sow financially into something directed by God.

Serpent: Satan, the ungodly kingdoms of this world, cunning and demonic, deception, curses, witchcraft. (For more information, see chapters 6–8.)

Sex: possibly a spirit of lust; the need for attention; if dreaming of a past relationship, there may be a need to cut soul ties; chronic dissatisfaction.

Shadow: God covering, overshadowing and protecting you; a time of healing (Peter's shadow); if dark, it may represent evil or death assignments.

Shark: hidden danger, evil predator approaching, stalking spirit.

Sheep: children of God, innocence, lack of wisdom, potential scattering.

Sheepdog: evangelism, protection.

Shelves: the need to put away old relationships, emotions, feelings, etc.; the need to put something on the shelf or take something off the shelf for use.

Shepherd: Jesus Christ, a literal pastor who may need prayer.

Shield: putting on the armor of God, the need for faith to arise.

Ships: a large ministry or organization.

Shoe: needing divine intervention concerning your spiritual walk, needing peace (the Gospel of peace), walking out one's destiny.

Shopping: making important decisions and choices, fulfilling a need.

Shoulder: responsibility, governmental authority, shouldering a heavy burden.

Showering: see *bathing.*

Silver: being purified, going through the fire, redemption.

Sirens: clear warning that danger or a battle is coming, a clarion call to prayer, an urgent need.

Sister: oneself, actual sister, spiritual sister, the Church.

Skiing: God's grace empowering you to move past life's disappointments.

Sky: God's covering and protection, seeing into the heavenly realm, God's presence.

Slavery: sin, bondage, addiction.

Sled: see *skiing.*

Sleep: the actual need to rest, need for a spiritual awakening.

Smoking: addictions, ungodly lifestyle, rebellion.

Snakes: see also *serpent*; in most cases represents something negative; deception; snare; entrapment; beguilement.

> **Green snakes:** Green often represents the soul realm, encompassing the intellect, mind and reasoning. Because green also represents peace, a green snake might represent a false sense of peace.

> **White snakes:** White represents purity and righteousness; a white snake may symbolize false righteousness. This is probably the result of self-righteous feelings by act or deed rather than the pure blood of Christ.

> **Black snakes:** Black most often represents failures, death, doubt, unbelief and lack or poverty. A black snake indicates a seductive spirit that speaks lies, causing God's children to doubt their spiritual inheritance of blessings and abundant life.

Yellow snakes: Yellow speaks of cowardice, but it is also the color of jealousy and hatred. The serpent here is slyly seducing its victims into hating and despising each other through jealousy.

Brown snakes: Brown most often speaks of the flesh and unclean things. A brown snake reveals unclean thoughts and actions along with fleshly desires.

Python: This snake uses its size and power to squeeze life from its victims. It is usually docile and passive after its appetite is satisfied, but when hungry it will quickly overpower its prey. It symbolizes witchcraft, divination, mindsets and religious spirits that prevent a move of God's Spirit.

Snow: times of disappointment (breakthroughs seem "frozen"), a call to war/prayer.

Soap: the need for a spiritual cleansing.

Spider: evil, sin, false doctrine, deceiving spirits, snares, being caught in a trap/web of confusion.

Spoon: the need to be spoon-fed for a season.

Spring: new season, freshness, fresh start, refreshing, needed changes taking place.

Squatters: demonic forces attempting to steal your rightful inheritance in Christ, illegal authority.

Stairs/steps: different stages in life that take you to higher or lower places in the Spirit. If going up—promotion; if going down—demotion.

Storm: change coming (good or bad), disturbance, spiritual warfare.

Street names: Study the meanings of the street names and then pray over the revelation.

Strongman: a strong demonic spirit that requires binding and loosing (see Mark 3:27) for breakthroughs.

Stove: feeling as if you are on the back burner, put on hold.

Submarine: going underground, hidden, submission to authority.

Suicide: a shout for immediate help, doing something that continues to bring harm.

Summer: in the heat of affliction, in the heat of the battle, harvest, recreation, vacation and play, change of seasons.

Sun: Jesus Christ, the Son (Malachi 4:2)

Sunburn: spending quality and quantity time with the Son, Jesus Christ, and your heart burned within you as you spent time with the Lord.

Sunrise: beginning of a new day, a new season, His mercies are new every morning.

Sunset: a time to prepare to rest, the end of a season.

Swearing/cursing: words spoken by the accuser of the brethren, an unclean spirit.

Swimming: contending with opposition, desperately trying to remain afloat, self-effort, joy, fun, recreation.

Sword: using the sword of the Spirit (God's Word) during spiritual warfare, empowered by God to cut down enemies.

T

Table: agreement, communion, covenant, underhanded (under the table), hidden motives, a place to discuss issues and make future plans.

Tablet: God writing on the tablet of your heart, His Word being written on your heart.

Tailor: God adjusting your life, attitude and belief systems.

Tank (army): heavy warfare prayer needed for protection, the need to "tank up" on the Word.

Tape measure: Examine yourself to determine whether you measure up; measuring yours and others' deeds, character, skill and so on.

Tarantula: a territorial demonic stronghold, Jezebel, python, Behemoth, Leviathan.

Teacher: a literal teacher you have sat under, a pastor, a minister, Jesus Himself, the need to be taught or to "listen up."

Teeth: needing wisdom, watching your words.

Telephone: the need to communicate more with God and with others, God giving you a message.

Telescope: having a prophetic eye, the ability to see far off, a watchman on the wall in prayer and intercession, getting a closer look.

Television: sharing a vision (*tell*-a-vision), sharing and teaching revelation. Sometimes it indicates too much television in the natural, which interrupts time with God.

Termites: the enemy eating away at spiritual foundations, things in our lives that we cannot seem to get rid of or that never seem to go away, the need for deliverance.

Test: a time of the Lord testing the heart, learning the lessons of life that require great wisdom.

Thief: Satan, the enemy who is intent on stealing from you (John 10:10).

Thigh: covenant agreements (good and bad), seductions.

Thirst: experiencing a very dry season, spiritual thirst for Jesus, living water, needing to meet with the well of living water.

Thunder: hearing the voice of the Lord, God's voice in the midst of a storm.

Tick: a relationship that is sucking the life from you, exhaustion.

Tiger: danger ahead, unforeseen attack, untrustworthiness.

Titanic: need to change direction!

Tongue: powerful instrument in spiritual warfare holding the power of life and death (Proverbs 18:21; James 3:4–5), unruly lifestyle, rebellion, lies, deceit.

Tornado: warning of coming danger, spiritual warfare.

Traffic light: directions in life: red = stop, green = go, yellow = caution.

Train: God's glory unending (His train filled the Temple), unending love of God, continuing cycles, the Church, moving from one place in the Spirit to another, progress.

Train derailed: plans of God being thwarted due to demonic assignments, a call for prayer, loss of vision.

Treasure chest: hidden awards and revelation about to be revealed.

Tree: nations, people, righteousness, steadfastness, person or covering, the cross, false altars and false worship.

Tricycle: infant stages, effort of the self, striving, not having necessary resources for a large endeavor.

Trumpet: a call to war, God's prophets speaking, Christ's second coming, celebration.

Tunnel: hiding, darkness, inability to see properly, escape, hope (light at the end of the tunnel), hard season, having "tunnel vision."

Turban: a radical change in thinking (renew the mind), righteousness, needing a garment change because the accuser of the brethren is lying about your identity.

Turtle: moving too slowly, the need to slow down, protected, shy.

Twins: Elijah's double-portion anointing, needing to embrace the supernatural, elevated level of ministry.

U

UFO: visitations from angels (both godly and demonic), be watchful.

Umbilical cord: remaining attached to someone/something that needs to be cut off, codependency, being demonically influenced and attacked by an "Amorite" spirit (a demonic spirit that slays us with its evil words) and/or a "Hittite" spirit (a demonic spirit that terrorizes and causes fear; see Ezekiel 16:3–4).

Umbrella: God's protection from danger and the storms of life, properly equipped to deal with storms and difficult times, a covering (spiritual and physical).

Underground: demonic activity, an Absalom spirit at work, something unseen, the need for revelation of what is unseen.

Unicycle: the importance of remaining balanced in lifestyle and religious activity.

Uniform: prepared for battle, need to join a particular group, remaining in unity.

Upstairs: symbolic of the second heaven, where spiritual warfare takes place; seeing into the second and third heavens; the call to a higher level; climbing the ladder of success.

Urinating: the literal need to urinate, the need to be relieved from a particular pressure you are facing, feeling as if you are losing control.

V

Vacation: the need to rest, potential burnout ahead, needed time away.

Valentine: desiring a mate, love, your love for the Lord, being married to Christ.

Valley: feeling "low," a very low point in your life and/or ministry, needing God to prove that He truly is the God of the valleys, a time of preparation, being set apart for a specific reason.

Vampire: demonic spirit; a particular job, ministry or person that is sucking the life from you, draining you physically, mentally and spiritually; a codependent relationship.

Van: see *automobile.*

Vehicles: Automobiles, cars, buses, vans, etc. mostly speak of the "size" of a particular call or ministry.

Veil: something hidden awaiting to be revealed.

Vertigo: the need for balance in one's life, balancing one's schedule, feeling as if you are walking a tightrope and you are fearful of falling or making a wrong choice.

Veteran: a person highly trained in spiritual warfare.

Vine: Jesus, the Vine; growing in God as you feed on the Word and remain attached.

Volcano: unpredictable, uncontrollable anger, explosive temper.

Vulture: wicked and unclean spirit, spiritual attack of death, ravenous, a spirit that will pick you apart or devour you piece by piece.

W

Wading in water: being afraid to go deeper in God, being concerned about making the wrong choices, testing the waters.

Waiter: the need to be waiting on God, a position of serving and servanthood.

Waking: the need to awaken to a spiritual truth, a wake-up call.

Wall: "hitting a wall," hindrances to accomplishing divine destiny, being close to breakthrough yet opposed by strong demonic assignment.

Wallet: see *purse.*

War: spiritual warfare, a call to prayer concerning an actual war.

Washing: needed cleansing, holiness.

Watch: God's perfect timing, the need to watch over your words and prophecies, the need to become watchful.

Watchdog: God watching over His promises to you, the need for divine protection.

Water: a move of the Spirit, Jesus, the living water, washing of the Word, Holy Spirit, truth, instability (Peter being unstable as water).

Waves: a time of experiencing heavy storms, grief, waves of God's blessings.

Wedding: our marriage to Jesus, covenant.

Weeds: sins, needed cleansing of the heart and motives.

Whale: running from the call of God on one's life.

Whirlwind: God's methods concerning taking us "up" a level, God's presence, empowerment of the Holy Spirit.

Wilderness: see *desert.*

Wind: a powerful move of the Holy Spirit, doctrine, negative and demonic opposition.

Window: revelation, something hidden being revealed, the seer anointing, seeing beyond circumstances, exposure, an unguarded opening in which an enemy might enter.

Wine: Christ's blood shed for us, Holy Communion, covenant, fruit of the Spirit, intoxicant, being crushed or pressed.

Winter: a hard time in life, feeling dead, barrenness, isolation, desolation, chronic dissatisfaction, waiting.

Witch: a Jezebel spirit, witchcraft, an evil spirit, curses, barrenness.

Wolf: spirits of people who have the intent to destroy you, a predator, devourer, false teacher, false prophet.

Woman: the Church, compassion, nourishment, seduction, Jezebel, helper.

Woods: feeling lost, inability to find one's way, needing help and counsel.

Wool: having the wool pulled over the eyes, deception, the need for warmth, comfort, needed relationships.

Wrestling: in a battle with God or others, striving, deliverance, opposition, tribulation, trying to gain control.

Writing: writing and expressing words that you never had an opportunity to say, a time to pay attention to God's messages to you.

X

Xerox: being a "copycat," a lack of self-confidence, needing to know your true identity in Christ, the need for the Lord to repeat something in a dream/message due to its importance, repeating a cycle over and over, generational cycles and curses.

X-ray: having a very high level of spiritual discernment, something that is being exposed, an internal issue that needs a spiritual/physical diagnosis and prognosis, a closer look at a particular problem.

Y

Yawning: deliverance that is taking place, dissatisfaction, unfulfilled dreams and boredom.

Yeast: the need to "rise" up, empowering others to rise up and operate in their spiritual gifting,

being "puffed up" and prideful, Pharisee.

Yoke: heavy burden, being in bondage, being in agreement (good and bad).

Z

Zebra: looking at something with a black-and-white perspective, no compromise, being prophetic.

Zion: the dwelling place of God; God, our fortress; place of covenant and godly worship.

Zipper: a sign to zip up your lips, remain silent concerning your opinions, watching over your words.

Zodiac signs: demonic guidance, witchcraft, being led by falsehoods.

10

The Dream That Saved My Life

*I*t was four o'clock in the morning, and I was feverishly polishing furniture and vacuuming the house. Once again, a sudden burst of energy followed the euphoria from the latest round of diet pills. Though I weighed only 78 pounds, the anorexic way of life demanded losing more and more weight if at all possible. A skeleton-thin body was not enough to stop this demonically induced oppression.

I was addicted to the drugs. Without them I would plunge even deeper into severe depression. Taking them regularly meant that eventually I would need more than before to get the same effect. I had already resorted to doing whatever I had to do to get the pills—I stole them from the pharmacy or stole money from anyone, anywhere I could, in order to ensure my supply. It was my only way of enduring the hunger pains and diverting my thoughts. The cycle of diet pills, vomiting and laxatives was consuming my time, my strength and, actually, my entire life. It *was* my life!

Days, even weeks, were consumed with laxative abuse and vomiting. I would be unable to leave the house due to the sudden urges triggered by the laxatives. If my life was not absolutely confined by the laxatives, the cycles of bingeing and purging weakened me to the point that I could not get out of bed. Only the false sense of "security strength" that came from the drugs got me through each day.

I managed to keep these things hidden from my family. I know that sounds impossible, but I was a very convincing liar. I told my loved ones that I had a rare virus that made me sick (and, as Mrs. Drama Queen, I especially overdid it to my husband). They believed me—probably because I *looked* sick!

My desperate need for control ruled my every choice. I was unable to control my environment to ensure emotional safety. I was unable to risk more rejection or abandonment; therefore, I isolated myself. Controlling my weight appeared to be the only thing I was able to accomplish well. I could lose weight better than anyone I knew. I took pride in this accomplishment and felt as if I were in total control. The truth, however, was that anorexia had control of me.

I did not care if I lived or died. The doctors told me that if I did not begin to eat, I *would* die. But being thin and in control was more important. I was completely absorbed with my bizarre behavior, and I had no intention of changing my lifestyle, even if it meant death.

I grabbed the polishing cloth and said to myself, "I'll clean this entire house until it sparkles!" Perfectionism was another area in which I took great pride. Little Miss Perfect, I was— perfect house, perfectly organized kitchen, perfectly clean bathrooms, closets, pantry . . . on and on it went. Yet the harder I tried to be perfect, the less perfect I became. This night, though, I was on a roll. Several speed pills and I was rocking and rolling through the house, armed with Windex, furniture polish and paper towels.

"Mommy!"

My daughter, Kim, was screaming. "Mommy!" she called with even more intensity. My hair stood on end! I rushed into my bedroom, where Kim was sleeping. Mickey was a firefighter at the time, and he was working a 24-hour shift that night. Kim jumped at the opportunity to sleep in Mom's bed any time she was allowed. This was one of those nights.

"Kim, what's wrong?" No answer. I turned on the light; she was asleep. I saw that her pillow was wet with tears. Still asleep, she cried out once more.

"Mommy! Mommy! Please don't die!"

I sat next to her in the bed. "Kim, wake up! Mommy's right here." I gently began to shake her into reality. "Kim, wake up. I'm right here." Kim opened her big blue eyes in disbelief. She grabbed hold of my thin, frail body in a desperate attempt to never let me go.

"What is wrong, honey? Did you have a bad dream?"

"Mommy, please don't go! Don't leave me! I need you, Mommy!" She was convinced I was going away, so I tried to reassure her.

"Honey, Mommy's right here."

"No, no," Kim cried out. "That man in the sky said you would be leaving. He said you would die. Please don't die, Mommy! Please don't die!"

Still convinced her hysteria was the result of a nightmare, I assured her once again I was not leaving. I stroked her hair, saying, "Mommy is right here," and comforted her by holding her closely to my body. "What man in the sky told you that?" I asked.

"That man! That man in the sky! The man in the sky you have been telling me about. You know, Mommy—Jesus! He told me that you were going to die, and I need you here with me, Mommy!" She began to cry again, holding me more tightly than before.

My heart sank as tears welled in my eyes. My lips quivered uncontrollably. I knew that God had spoken to my young daughter in her dream in an attempt to reach me. He was not trying to frighten my daughter or cause her to feel abandoned. He was trying to reach *me*. The Lord is so wise that He knew that if I could not live for myself, I would fight to live for her. *No one else could love her as much as I do*, I thought. *I am her mother, and my daughter has a destiny in God to fulfill. I am the privileged one the Lord chose to birth her and rear her.* A desire to fight for life arose within me.

For the very first time, I *wanted* to live! I could not bear leaving my child, as the Lord knew. I would not fight for *my* life, but I *would for her*.

"Kim, I promise you," I vowed, "Mommy is not leaving you. Mommy will *never* leave you." I knew the vow I made was a fixed one. For years I had wasted away under a death curse, a slow attempt at suicide. Now, supernaturally, the breath of hope and life filled me. I knew I could survive this devastating bout with anorexia and bulimia, for God had spoken to me through my daughter. For the first time, I heard His voice *through a dream*.

This began my journey into full recovery. It was not an easy road; I had many hidden emotional addictions to work through. Issues of control had to be faced. Deep-seated inadequacies, fears of failure and fears of rejection were singled out and worked through with professional counselors. Most importantly I realized that the hand of God was in total control. But it was not until I began to have dreams of deliverance that I experienced the full freedom I had desired.

Deliverance Is for Us All

Many believers do not believe in the necessity of deliverance. It is my personal belief that, although Christians cannot be "possessed" by demons, due to choices we have made and generational strongholds we can certainly be influenced and affected by them. My heart's desire is not to stir up a theological debate concerning this issue; I am simply giving my personal testimony, what I know to be true concerning my need for deliverance from much demonic oppression. Before you decide that deliverance is not for you, let me explain how the Scripture defines *deliverance*. After you read this, pray over it and take it to heart; I am certain you will reach out to the Lord for more freedom yourself!

In the Bible, the word translated "deliverance" is the Hebrew word *teshuw'ah*, meaning "to rescue." It is further translated to mean "help, safety, salvation and victory." Its root, *shava*, means "to be free," and it is used to describe freedom from trouble. It is also connected to a Hebrew word that means "to cry out." Believer, I needed freedom! I needed to be rescued, and I was crying out for the Lord to help me. I am grateful that He chose to answer me with dreams that opened doors for complete deliverance.

I firmly believe that He desires to give you dreams also that will ultimately set you forever free. As you continue to read, I believe that your hope is rising. God desires to heal your heart, set you free and show His divine love to you as well. Before we move forward, let me end this chapter with a New Testament example of Christ's desire to deliver us. In Luke 4:18–19 (KJV, emphasis added), we read that Jesus came not only to preach the Gospel and heal the brokenhearted, but to preach deliverance and bring them liberty:

> The Spirit of the Lord is upon me, because he hath anointed me to preach the gospel to the poor; he hath sent me to heal the brokenhearted, to preach *deliverance* to the captives, and recovering of sight to the blind, to set at liberty them that are bruised, to preach the acceptable year of the Lord.

In this New Testament passage, the Greek word for "deliverance" is *aphesis*, meaning "freedom and pardon." It is further translated to mean "forgiveness, liberty and remission."

When God delivered me from my disease and near-death assignments, He also forgave me! He gave me the gift of liberty and freedom from my slavery mentality. I was in sin, and He chose to forgive me and set me completely free. Dear one, He promises to do the same for you. Yes, God is in your future, and He sees you completed—I like to tell people, "He's back from the future!" Many of your dreams will be revelation that will open the doors to your future, your freedom and your life of victory!

In the coming chapters you will read more of my personal testimony concerning my deliverance from the premature death assignment—deliverance that came through God-given dreams and visions. I am excited and confident that the Holy Spirit is speaking to you as we continue this journey together. Turn the page and expect an impartation from heaven that will empower you to experience all that heaven has to offer! You will never consider your dreams worthless again.

11

Deliverance through Dreams

*B*eloved, it is true: God wants us to be free! Look at what the Word says concerning freedom: "And ye shall know the truth, and the truth shall make you free. . . . If the Son therefore shall make you free, ye shall be free indeed" (John 8:32, 36 KJV).

Most of the time, to heal us emotionally, spiritually and physically, God will reveal the strongholds that continually oppress His children. Many physical and emotional problems are the result of demonic oppression. Mine definitely was! Through revelation, God begins to expose His truth so that we may be completely free. Therefore, knowing, seeing and agreeing with the truth will release us from demonic activity.

I want to assure you that God's truth is often revealed through dreams and visions. To *not* receive the dreams and visions that God gives you is to refuse truth, the very thing Christ came to give us. By embracing what the Lord releases through prophetic revelations and dreams, the Body of Christ can move to a new level in the Spirit. Dreams and visions are part of the "strong meat" that Paul mentioned in Hebrews 5:14 (KJV): "But strong meat belongeth to them that are of full age, even those who by reason of use have their senses exercised to discern both good and evil." Only those who are mature in the Spirit are able to digest strong meat. It requires laying aside childish ways, including mindsets and tradition, and growing up in God. It also requires that His children no longer come into agreement with the lies of Satan.

For many years I believed the complete opposite of what God's Word states concerning me. Before I received deliverance, I believed lies—lies that I was unworthy, shameful, rejected and abandoned. I was performance oriented and emotionally handicapped in every possible way. Death seemed to be my only escape . . . and you might say that I wanted to die because I was certainly dying on the inside! Thank God that He reached out and touched me—and delivered me.

We are in a season when God is restoring His people. The word *restore* means "to be safe," "to be in covenant," "to be at peace" and "to be complete." God wants us whole and complete. Part of our destiny is to operate in our godly giftings; if there is no fulfillment of destiny, then we will suffer from being incomplete and unfulfilled. Our potential lies dormant until activated by the Holy Spirit. At that point, God desires that each individual walk in the fullness of His calling (Ephesians 3:19).

The Lord promised restoration in order for us to receive hope and peace through the power of the Holy Spirit. Restoration also implies that there is a *rebuilding* of the walls, bringing back the glory of God into our lives. For me, when God began to restore, He began to rebuild the walls of my life. Walls of defense against my enemies (fear, doubt, unbelief, insecurity and abandonment) were erected by the power of the Holy Spirit. No longer could my enemies gain entrance into my life. The days of plunder into my land (my life) by Satan and his cohorts were over!

My Personal Deliverance through Dreams

As I mentioned in the previous chapter, deliverance implies *freedom and liberation*. Freedom is available for every child of God. It was a few years after Kim's dream that I found myself seduced back into the same anorexic behavior. I tried over and over and over to break completely free—yet a residue of the anorexic lifestyle would always emerge. I needed deliverance; I needed more help, but I could find no one to help me. Coming from a denominational background in which the people did not believe in the gifts of the Holy Spirit, I did not understand what was available. Sunday after Sunday I would approach the altar, begging God to help me progress. I had tried with all my might to fully recover, only to propel backward again. My weight had stabilized at ninety pounds, but I still frequented the old habits of laxative and drug abuse. I was older now, weary and worn down from the emotional and physical struggle. Mine had been a seven-year battle with anorexia, bulimia, death wishes and struggles for survival and wholeness. I was surviving—but barely. Then, in one night, breakthrough came!

The Phone Call

"Sissy!" My sister, Pam, was on the line when I picked up the phone. Besides my husband, she had been my strength. Pam has always believed in me, no matter what. (Thank the Lord for such a wonderful, loyal sister!)

"Are you watching the news? Karen Carpenter has died from anorexia!"

Chills ran down my spine. In great disbelief, I refuted her statement. "No! Not Karen Carpenter!" I responded as if Karen Carpenter had been my friend. But actually, for the first time, I was facing the full reality that people really do die from anorexia. I had always admired Karen Carpenter; I could relate to her as a person, and I could relate to her illness and, now, her death. I felt the shock of her passing as though it had happened to me. Her musical recordings and distinct singing style began churning in my memory, bringing me back to events in high school and college. Then, it happened. The audible voice of God got my full attention because He loves me so.

You will be next if you don't turn this behavior around NOW.

God's words shook me to the foundation of my soul. Suddenly, before my eyes opened up a vision of my own funeral. I saw an open casket, and I was lying in it! Flowers surrounded the casket and filled the church. This was not my imagination—it was undeniably an open vision. God literally came crashing into my world . . . once again revealing the condition of my heart. In the vision, I completely understood that I really could die if I did not shift; I also realized my backslidden condition with God. My heart raced with the fearful reality of the consequences.

Suddenly, I knew that I knew: *This was it!* No more "trying." No more "wanting to be free"! This was my *kairos* moment for transformation, and I needed to *choose life!* I did not understand what a *kairos* moment was, but I knew that it was my time to shift into a new place with God. Now that I understand the times and seasons of God, I understand better what was happening then: Up until that moment I had been experiencing *chronos* time—the normal, day-to-day grind of life. It is the natural passing of time, the day-in and day-out routine. We walk through life believing and hoping God is leading us. We believe in His promises and make small shifts in our lifestyles along the way. All the while we are hoping, believing and applying faith that one day, as He promises, we will get the breakthrough. Suddenly comes the major shift into our destiny; we have experienced the *kairos* moment of change. *Kairos* time brings with it a significant change in our lives that affects history.

One can compare this process to a woman who is pregnant with child. Her *chronos* time is the season of carrying the child in the womb. Each morning the mother wakes up and fulfills her daily responsibilities, knowing that her season to deliver has not arrived. For nine months she dwells in *chronos* time. Then, suddenly, the labor pains begin. The time has come for a shift in her life. No longer will she simply carry the child in the womb; soon she will experience the child from the perspective of an active, responsible mother. After the birth, different responsibilities will be required. The birthing process will be painful; it will require endurance and determination. Then, suddenly, as the baby comes forth . . . the *kairos* moment occurs! The birth has come; history is changed and a new life has been born. It was the same for me the moment I heard God's audible voice. No longer could I remain the same.

Because of the divine encounter, hearing God's voice and seeing an open vision, I fully embraced the direction of change. Finally, I shifted into a permanent place of *life*! From that moment forward I never struggled with the bondage of the anorexic lifestyle again. I was never tempted to "go back" to the old ways. I would never return to the leeks and garlic of Egypt, praise the Lord!

The moment God sent His Word through a heavenly vision, I was changed. I instantly had a new heart and became a new person. Though I still suffered deep emotional scars, I knew I had the victory over that oppressive lifestyle. Now I could advance into my God-given destiny. I still had to journey through a process of deliverance and counseling, but the chains of bondage had been broken. I was finally free to experience the fullness of freedom that Christ offered through the finished work at the cross.

Getting Off the Merry-Go-Round

I have to be honest and say that, at times during my journey, I felt like I was on a merry-go-round. Do you ever feel that you are going around and around the very same mountain? I have been that route myself.

A few years after that divine encounter and my shift, I developed a viral infection that led me, once again, close to death. Again doctors said I would die if I was not healed. I had finally gotten over the anorexic lifestyle, and now a potentially fatal viral infection threatened to do me in! Could it be any clearer that the enemy wanted to destroy me? It was indeed becoming very clear—and I cried out for more divine intervention.

I was battling once again for my life, and I became discouraged in the battle. I was not feeling any different, I was still in pain and I suffered under very high fevers. It felt as if I were losing ground rather than gaining it. No sign of victory seemed to be manifesting in the natural. I warred with many prophetic promises, as Paul had told Timothy to do (1 Timothy 1:18 AMPC) . . . and somehow maintained my faith. But I desperately needed to see some change. Though I was no longer anorexic, I now faced death again if I did not witness a miracle in my body. I said to myself, "I feel like I am on a merry-go-ground and I can't get off!" After saying that, I lay down and instantly fell asleep to receive a very encouraging dream.

The merry-go-round dream. In the dream, I was trying to push through a door. I knew that if I could push past the closed door, life, healing and complete freedom awaited me on the other side. While I pushed, I saw Satan's arm holding the door closed. I would push forward, and he would push the door back in my face.

Then the scene changed, and suddenly I burst through the door. I was driving a bumper car, similar to bumper cars at a carnival. When I had pushed through the door, right in front of me was a merry-go-ground in full motion. Amazingly, I observed Satan being firmly seated on one of its horses! As I steered the bumper car, I drove up onto the carousel. As I began to drive the bumper car on the carousel, I began to push the carousel horses out of the way. Every blockage was completely mowed down by the bumper car I was driving! Satan turned around and looked at me—and *he* had fear on his face! I woke up with great excitement—*he* was afraid of *me*! No longer was I fearful of him and his tactics; now he was terrorized by me!

Once awake, I sought the Lord for the interpretation. The door was the place of my freedom. The carousel represented "going around the mountain again"—in other words, I was dealing with attacks from Satan again. The bumper car symbolized that *no weapon formed against me is going to prosper.* As you probably know, bumper cars are heavily padded, and any impact on the car is deflected away due to the cushioning around it. The Lord showed me that the bumper car was my anointing! My life, my hope, my strength were in the anointing of God. As long as I was flowing and moving in that, the devil had no place in my life. My connection was to stay in the safe place of anointing. Most exciting was that the Lord was revealing that a future victory over the devil was very real and tangible!

The Devil Is Real—but Victory Is Promised

Dear one, again, I shared that experience and dream to encourage you. Many of us have been speaking to mountains and commanding them to be gone! Yet many of those mountains are actually demons and demonic oppression. Jesus even referred to a mountain as a demon in Matthew 17:14–20 (KJV), when He was instructing His disciples concerning doubt and unbelief. The devil is a liar and is no match for the Lord. Have faith today. You have enough faith at this very moment to receive healing and deliverance. Speak to whatever is opposing you right now! Job 22:28 says that we can make a decree and whatever we decree becomes established. In closing this chapter, let's examine this passage carefully: "You shall also decide and decree a thing, and it shall be established for you; and the light [of God's favor] shall shine upon your ways" (Job 22:28 AMPC).

When we make a decree, we are speaking forth a type of declaration. The Hebrew word for "decree" in this passage is *gazar*, a primitive root word meaning "to cut down or off, (figuratively) to destroy, divide, exclude, or decide." Dear believer, think about it. When you declare God's Word and speak forth His promises concerning your life and future, you are cutting off the voice of the enemy. Yes! When you decree your promises, you cut down the enemy; you cut off his plans and you exclude yourself from them. Isn't that awesome?

Go ahead—cry out to God right now. Make a decree and declare your salvation! Declare your freedom and victory in Christ. Freedom is *today*!

In the next chapter you will read about the generational strongholds that were revealed to me through a series of dreams. God's faithfulness to continue to speak during the night seasons opened the door for Sandie Freed to become completely freed!

12

My Generational Journey to Freedom

*P*recious reader, you now know many of the divine encounters I have had as I traveled the road to freedom and health. But they did not end there. After recovering from anorexia and bulimia, I still battled a spirit of death. I needed something more to make a final and complete shift: I needed keys to unlock my freedom.

When I finally broke free from the destructive lifestyle, I turned my attention to finding everything needed for a complete release from roots of infirmity, rejection and abandonment. The spirits of rejection and infirmity were so intertwined into my personality and lifestyle, they required a seriously concentrated effort to break free from their entanglement. I continued to struggle with perfectionism, fear of man and performance. Though I was ministering under the anointing and power of the Holy Spirit, even witnessing miracles, I still dealt with identity problems.

Desperate once again, I cried out for more deliverance. Again, God answered my prayers . . . this time through not just one dream but a series of dreams. At first, I could not piece them together, because I did not yet have the full interpretations. Through patience and persistence, however, the truth began to unfold through the Holy Spirit. Dream after dream about generational curses provided the keys I needed to open the doors of deliverance.

The First Key: The Birthday Dream

September 1 is my birthday. For years, I was either in the hospital during the month of September or sick on or immediately following my birthday. In fact, before my release from generational curses, I honestly cannot remember a month of September when I was not ill. Obviously, a curse of death was released on my life the day I was born, and for some reason that curse (empowered by a demon of premature death) tried to collect each year on my birthday! One night, on August 31, I prayed for a dream. I asked the Lord to reveal the stronghold holding me captive to this spirit of premature death. Anorexia was over—but what was the root? God was once again faithful and answered my prayer. Around one o'clock in the morning of my birthday came the dream that gave me the first key needed for deliverance.

> **Dream of the birthday card.** In the dream, I began to open a birthday card. It appeared to be a standard card, nothing alarming and nothing unusual on the cover. The outside read very simply, "Happy Birthday." Upon opening the card, however, I was alarmed to read the words, "Just to let you know, I have the right to be here." The card was signed, "Satan."

I awoke startled and confused. *Satan has a right to be in my life?* I thought. *And He is remembering my birthday?* Within a few minutes I understood that a generational assignment against my life had been released from the time I was in the womb. When I was born, the enemy came to divert God's purpose for my life. It was what I refer to as a "demonic birth assignment." Satan still had a right, a legal entrance, to remain in control of my life.

I was of Native American heritage, and, through much research on Creek Indian culture, I realized curses were attached to my bloodline. Exodus 20:5 (AMPC) says this concerning the generations:

> You shall not bow down yourself to them or serve them; for I the Lord your God am a jealous God, visiting the iniquity of the fathers upon the children to the third and fourth generation of those who hate Me.

The iniquity of the fathers can give Satan a legal right to influence their descendants to the third and fourth generation. What iniquity had been committed by my fathers that gave Satan that right in my life? The time had come to pray and ask the Lord to reveal more concerning generational assignments and the legal ground Satan possessed. My crying out led to more dreams that disclosed secrets of Satan's kingdom and his plans to oppress my life.

I discerned that the death assignment had an open door in my life through my Native American heritage—a potent connection to my family line. My great-grandfather (through my father's mother) was a Creek Indian who was recognized as a prominent authority figure within his tribe. He was also highly recognized by people not of Native American descent. He was so influential that a city in Oklahoma is named after him and my great-grandmother.

My great-grandfather also clearly had a prophetic gift that was passed down to me as his descendant. He was known by many in the area as one who "knew where other people's horses were"—just as Samuel was able to tell Saul where to find his donkeys (see 1 Samuel 9:19–20). He also had the ability to "see" economic opportunity that opened the door to industry and brought prosperity to his town. At the same time, idolatry, mysticism and witchcraft were prevalent in his tribe, and these things opened the door for the enemy to gain a foothold in his descendants.

The generational lineage through my father's father was rooted in even more witchcraft. My great-grandmother was a séance leader and held séances in her house, calling upon evil spirits and communicating with the dead. She operated in the supernatural by a familiar spirit.

When I was in my mother's womb, my mother attended one of the séances. (This was before any of us knew the Lord forbade such things!) My great-grandmother "prophesied" over my mother's womb (with *me* in it), saying, "The child that you have will be very gifted" (implying gifted in the supernatural). I later realized that I had been marked for Satan's kingdom.

Dear reader, listen up, because you will find this interesting. When I was a child, I had many demonic visitations, dreams and visions of demons. I would awake from these encounters screaming in fear. It seemed as if I could actually see the demons manifest. I now believe, however, that I was having visions and visions within dreams. Upon my awakening or coming out of a vision, my parents would rush to help me . . . but they blamed it all on my vivid imagination. As a result, I grew up with emotional scars from these occurrences. I felt misunderstood and abandoned by my parents' lack of interest in what was occurring in the night seasons. Nightmares plagued me through most of my childhood.

Only much later did I realize the varied aspects of my family history had invited demonic activity and a premature death assignment into my life. It was my generational heritage that released the torment, fear and rejection that plagued me—the result of iniquity in my lineage. Yes, I was marked for the kingdom of darkness through witchcraft and a familiar spirit. These would have to be broken off in order for me to step into life and freedom.

The Second Key: The Generational Line

Though set free from anorexic eating patterns and severe bouts with weight loss, I had lingering areas in my soul that needed sanctification. I had been through deliverance with anointed ministers, yet in some areas I still needed healing. I realized that Scripture states that *little by little* God would drive away the beasts from my field (see Deuteronomy 7:22).

I was determined to be completely free, so each night I would give the Lord control of my thoughts and ask for a dream. I trusted God enough to know that through a dream He would reveal the hidden areas that withheld my breakthroughs. On my journey toward wholeness, I continued receiving these dreams, and more revelation began to unfold concerning generational curses and strongholds. Each dream proved to be a key to complete deliverance.

Dream of the desolate place. In one dream, I was in a desolate place. I saw myself standing in front of a firing squad. Sweat dripped from my forehead onto the blindfold that covered my eyes. With my hands tied behind me, I was unable to avoid the irritating sweat, and I desperately desired to remove the blindfold in order to see my assailants. The material, which held my eyes captive, was thin enough to see through. I continually strained to focus on the line forming before me. The firing squad was composed of generations of my family, with my relatives forming a line, one behind the other.

Each member of my family took a place in line, awaiting the opportunity to execute me. I was not alarmed as I identified my executioners. Though they were my family, it seemed normal and expected that they be the ones to terminate my life.

The first family member in line took the gun and aimed at my forehead. The others in line were calmly waiting their turn to do the same, knowing that they would soon be passing the gun to the others. Taking turns to further inflict the punishment was part of the judgment due to my guilt. Very confidently, my first assassin took aim and pulled the trigger; I observed the bullet as it was released from the chamber. It shot forth in very slow motion. Each second was tormenting as I awaited the impact of the blow of death. I closed my eyes, not able to watch any longer.

"God!" I cried out inside myself, "Help me!" The dream ended.

When I awoke, I was sitting straight up in bed. My heart was racing. The bed was soaked from nervous sweat due to the intensity of the dream. The dream was so real I could not get my physical bearings. Finally, as my heart began beating at a slower pace, I was able to comprehend what God had just revealed in the dream.

The interpretation came immediately, and it proved to be a key that was needed to unlock another door leading to my freedom: The long line of family members was the lineage through which the generational curse came through my father's line. The death spirit had a legal right to come through the sins of my forefathers—specifically my Native American heritage, which opened the door to the curse of idolatry and witchcraft in me. The idolatry, mysticism and witchcraft practiced by my ancestors gave Satan a legal right to be in my life. I was constantly tormented with fear and fear of death along with ongoing illness.

The Third Key: Final Deliverance

The Lord does not always open doors in your life overnight. Often, it requires Him revealing clues and symbols, and you must apply research, all while being led by the Holy Spirit. Because of so many dreams concerning my heritage, I decided to travel to Muskogee, Oklahoma, to investigate that heritage at the Creek Nation Museum. (A key to uncovering the mysteries of your heritage may require a trip to a library or museum.) During this time, I began to have a series of dreams containing mounds of dirt, similar to huge ant hills.

Mickey and I drove to Oklahoma, and as we approached the museum, I recognized huge mounds of dirt beside the building. I had no idea what these mounds represented in my dreams. I later learned that the Creek Indians formed their burial grounds with enormous mounds of dirt. I began to understand the strategies of the spirit of death through this revelation.

While praying and asking God for direction in Oklahoma, I had the dream that proved to be the final key I needed.

Dream of the green corn ceremony. In the dream, I saw myself walking through a field, and green corn appeared everywhere. I saw green kernels and stalks of corn as far as the eye could see. I saw my Creek ancestors gathering together in a time of great harvest. The ancestors were celebrating and eating the green corn. I began to hide behind bushes to observe this bizarre behavior. End of dream.

After I awoke, I searched the Bible for the symbolism of green corn. I found nothing that I felt related to the dream. I knew corn usually represented a time of fruitfulness or a harvest; at the time, however, I did not feel a harvest applied because God was taking me through deliverance. Yet I knew that God was exposing something—obviously, things had been hidden from me. The devil did not want me to understand the strongholds established through the sins of the generations that came before me; this is why I felt I needed to "hide" in the dream. As I prayed, revelation slowly came forth.

Remember the importance of the month of September in my life? It seemed as if almost every September I had a dream concerning Indians, but every September I was also deathly ill. While at the museum I wanted to locate the keys that would unlock the mystery behind the bondage I continued to experience around the time of my birthday. Desperately seeking specific books, articles and any documentation, I asked God to reveal a key needed for my freedom.

It was not difficult locating information about my great-grandfather; he was so prominent that there were articles on his life and family in the museum. In fact, at one time his rifle, his picture and artifacts from our family were encased for visitors to observe. I finally located a book documenting specific facts concerning the Creek Indians. I thumbed through the table of contents and found a chapter entitled, "Green Corn Ceremony."

In my excitement, I could barely wait to locate the pages! To my surprise, I learned that *every year in August and September the Creek Indians would celebrate a corn festival to a false god*. Idolatry was proven in my heritage, and I knew that the consequences of idolatry always involved a generational curse. Also during the months of August and September, the Creek Indians would drink a potion that would cause them to vomit for three solid days to purge themselves. Keep in mind that I not only had anorexia, I was also bulimic. There were days that I did nothing but eat and throw up. Although I had not exhibited this behavior in years, I wanted revelation of the *root* so the behavior would never return and the curse of death could be broken.

Dear one, this dream was key to my breakthrough. The purging that my ancestors did during this ceremony was to "rid" them of their shame! I had dealt with a stronghold of shame since I was a child. Now, with the revelation in this dream I was able to finally break free!

My past is difficult to admit to others, but I want to give you confidence that God cares about you, too . . . He wants us to be free. Christ has come to set us free: "If the Son therefore shall make you free, ye shall be free indeed" (John 8:36 KJV). Yes! The Lord revealed the roots of my anorexic death behavior, and I got excited as the truth began to set me free. The spirit of death was not the only thing that came through my Creek heritage—so did the anorexic and bulimic spirit. I related to my husband the connection between my dreams and all that God revealed. We began to pray and to break the death assignment.

I was finally free! And my complete freedom came through the voice of God in the night season. It has been many years now that I have not dealt with an illness on my birthday. I was delivered because of the Word of the Lord delivered through my dream.

God cares so much about you that He will bring deliverance keys to you while you sleep. Dear one, He delivered me. He set me free. He healed my mind and my body. Nothing is impossible with God (Matthew 19:26; Mark 10:27). And, precious one, He wants to do the same for you. Yes, keep dreaming!

13

God Is Speaking to Our Children

*O*ur gifted younger generation is anointed and wired for the supernatural. In more than thirty years of pastoring, I have been amazed at the hundreds of testimonies I have heard of children having godly dreams and visions. It is obvious to me that God desires to make Himself known to our children in a very personal way. Unfortunately, many have held belief systems that deny God's desire to speak to us—especially to our children. But regardless of what we think, we have a relentless God who wants to draw all of us near to develop an intimate relationship with Him.

Our children are designed and created for Kingdom activity and Kingdom purpose. They are designed to rule and reign in Christ; thus many of their dreams point to opportunities for them to develop their godly identities. In this chapter, I want to address God's desire to speak to our children through dreams and visions and His desire that your child rule and reign in Christ . . . *even at a young age!* We have been unaware and uneducated as to *how* to help our children grow in this, especially in the following areas:

- Hearing from God through dreams and visions.
- Understanding that dreams and visions are often from God.
- Benefitting from a vision or dream.
- Dealing with nightmares and turning them around to experience peace and victory.

It is my hope and intent to help you find the answers you need to help your children in these areas. I want to encourage and empower you to help your children understand the value of their dreams and visions. This book may be written for adults, but many of the truths and testimonies in it apply to the lives of children, too, and they can encourage and empower you to become a "life coach" to your own children as they encounter God in dreams and visions. (And, yes, I understand that parents have to use wisdom and verbiage appropriate for the ages of their children; know that I have taken that into account throughout this chapter.) So use what you have already learned, and have an open mind and heart as we finish this journey together. God wants to use your children for His glory just as much as He desires to use you!

Children Who Hear God's Voice

Dear one, God is visiting your children in dreams. In chapter 10, you read how the Lord visited my daughter, Kim, in a dream and how that visitation saved my life. Your children are also being visited by Him because He loves them. When they are quiet and settled down at night, He will give them dreams and speak to them concerning their future. He will also reveal the truth behind fears, worries, cares of the day and much more.

And there *is* much more! The entire supernatural realm is open to our children. Angels are visiting our kids, just as they minister to us while we sleep. The Bible makes it clear that angels appear in dreams to give direction, just as they did with Joseph when he had wedded Mary. Several times an angel spoke directly to Joseph in dreams about where to take Jesus, the Son of God, to keep Him safe. Two thousand years ago, seeing angels was a common occurrence (in both dreams and in the natural)—and it should be now!

I have heard testimonies like this: A parent noticed her child talking to someone, but no one was there. The parent was concerned about the child talking to an imaginary friend, so she sought counsel from someone who could teach biblically on dreams and visions. That teacher instructed her to ask the child to whom he was talking. The child told the parent that he was talking to an angel!

Children in our congregation have told me they saw angels during a church service. Sadly, many times a parent would step in to say, "Oh, he has a vivid imagination!" Let me assure you, we need to pay attention when a child tells us he or she sees angels. Remember that children have enormous faith! They are not calloused, as many of us are, but innocent, and their eyesight reflects that they are full of faith. Let's be careful not to rebuke them when they describe angelic encounters, whether in a dream or in a vision.

Now, I understand that we as parents need to be discerning and not blithely give our assent when our children tell us they are talking to those who live in the supernatural realm! We need to be sure that our children are safe and that they are not actually talking to a demonic influence. But we must also not throw the baby out with the bathwater. How many times have our children said that an angel visited them and we have written it off as vivid imagination? What if I had done that when my own daughter dreamed of Jesus visiting her? Remember, He told her to tell me that I would die if I did not change! Whether children see an angel in a more literal vision or in a metaphoric dream, the experiences are in essence the same—supernatural encounters with the God who loves them. He loved my daughter (and me) enough to warn her about my future. Did it ever get my attention—thank God I believed her!

Do you remember how God called the young boy Samuel? In 1 Samuel 3, we read of God giving important messages to Samuel at a very young age. (The ancient Jewish historian Josephus records that he was just twelve years old!) When the Lord called out Samuel's name, however, he did not recognize God's voice, so he ran to his spiritual father, Eli. This happened three times before Eli finally perceived that the Lord Himself was attempting to communicate with the boy. This story is incredible and incredibly encouraging. Thinking of how God desires to visit us, even as children, brings tears to my eyes.

What if your son or daughter's story is Samuel's story? What if your child feels left out and unpopular, a victim of peer pressure and society's demands to achieve? What if the Lord is attempting to talk to him or her for encouragement and direction? When we read Samuel's account, we realize that Eli almost completely aborted his opportunity to teach his spiritual son how to hear the voice of God. It took three times for Eli to recognize that since *he* was not calling out Samuel's name, it was probably God. At that point Eli finally said to Samuel, "Go, lie down; and it shall be, if He calls you, that you must say, 'Speak, LORD, for Your servant hears'" (verse 9 NKJV). We, too, can become parents who listen, encourage and admonish our children in their destinies as revealed by the voice of the Lord.

Scripture notes that God actually "came and stood" in Samuel's vision and gave him a very important message concerning Eli's household. This is exactly how God may be speaking to your children—*in a vision!*

Then there is Joseph, the son of Jacob, to whom God began to speak in dreams when he was just seventeen. God saw fit to speak to Joseph with metaphoric imagery, even though he was young. Take some time to read the account of Joseph's dreams in Genesis 37:5–11 to notice the symbolism God used to communicate Joseph's future and destiny.

Discerning Your Children's Dreams

Even if our children have not received Jesus as Savior, God still desires to speak to them. After all, God does not speak only to Christians! Think about Saul, who became the apostle Paul, and how God spoke to him in a vision on the road to Damascus. Saul was considered to have an antichrist spirit, but God relentlessly pursued him! There are multitudes of testimonies of Muslims, Buddhists and people of other religions having dreams from God that led them to seek Jesus as their Savior.

On the other hand, we cannot assume that our dreams, nor our children's dreams, are all from the Lord. We must learn to discern their origins, as I taught in earlier chapters. Take some time to review those chapters to help you discern your child's dreams. To keep it simple, let's focus now on three main categories of dreams and visions our children have:

- *Dreams that are demonically inspired.* Demonically inspired dreams are extremely intense and frightening and are often considered nightmares. They can be in black and white, in color or in extremely vivid colors. In a bit, I will go into detail about these and explain how to stop them.
- *Dreams that are soul inspired.* Scripture gives clear warnings about dreams that originate in our own souls (see Jeremiah 29:8). This is because dreams of the soul are more about what *you* think, what *you* feel, because they involve your mind, will and emotions. These dreams are

often more muted in color, and they can involve selfish desires or ambitions.

- *Dreams that are God inspired.* Dreams inspired by God are usually in bright, true colors. They have a spiritual weight to them—inviting the dreamer to live a virtuous or more holy life—or are directive in some manner. I remember having dreams as a child about being a teacher. I later entered college to be a nurse, but I graduated as a teacher of four different subjects! This was a God-inspired dream.

  Remember, most dreams from God are given in metaphors and require interpretation. Seeking the interpretation with our children is considered a privilege (see Proverbs 25:2). Spend time in prayer for and with your children as you are seeking answers; this will empower them to hear more from God for themselves.

As you work with your children in understanding the purpose of dreams, remind them in age-appropriate language that

- He desires to communicate with them;
- He desires to lead and guide them;
- He desires to reveal areas in their lives that will distract them from fulfilling their destiny and purpose;
- He speaks often in a small, still voice through dreams; and
- He also speaks in visions.

Tool Kit for Successful Recall and Interpretation

As you spend time listening and encouraging your children in their dreams and visions, you will need a tool kit for success:

- Become extremely familiar with biblical accounts of dreams and visions. As you share these stories with your children, they will be encouraged to hear from God in the same manner and will go to sleep with an expectation of touching heaven in their night seasons.

- Journal each dream (this is important). Write down the date, give the dream a title and document the different symbols. Asking your children to draw a picture of different parts of the dream is helpful for recall. You will be surprised how much more they will remember when they write or draw! Even taking time for them to act out their dreams will be helpful. Psychiatrists have proven that role play empowers recall. Encourage them not to be intimidated but to act out the parts as best they are able. This will also release freedom and creativity.

- Pray with your children as you ask for the guidance of the Holy Spirit for the interpretation or message.

- Try your best to keep the main thing the main thing. Keep it as simple as possible as you explain the main symbols to your children.

- Review their dreams and visions periodically; I recommend at least every six months—but even better is to do it every quarter (three months).

As you invite your child to discover his or her world of dreams, you will discover a world of newfound adventure together. Interpreting dreams together invites quality time and intimacy. It is, of course, easy to interpret dreams when they involve someone like Spider-Man, the hero who saves the day. Cartoon characters reflect the roles children play and blend into desires a child might have, which are later expressed in dreams. Nightmares, on the other hand, are more difficult to interpret! Let's turn our attention now to how we as parents deal with the things that afflict and torment children most in the night seasons: nightmares and night scares.

Nightmares and Night Scares

No matter where my travels take me, I hear parents tell me
that their children are afraid to go to sleep because of their
nightmares. Nightmares, dear friend, are universal! I have also
found that every culture has its own way of dealing with dreams,
especially nightmares and night scares (also known as night
terrors). The Native Americans, for instance, ward off nightmares by hanging a device known as a dream catcher at the
end of the bed.

I remember my grandmother giving my parents a dream
catcher when she heard I was having horrible nightmares. In
fact, she offered them one that she had as a child! The Native
Americans believed that dream catchers caught bad dreams in
the web of the catcher, and that only the good dreams were
allowed to completely pass through. I am glad now that my
mother refused to use it, but at the time I begged for her to
hang it over my bed. I did not know that it would have been
asking for even more troubled dreams.

Now, I do not believe in dream catchers, because there are
effective, biblical ways to deal with spiritual threats to us and our
children. You already know my testimonies of nightmares and
demonic visitations (through demonic visions), and you have
seen how God empowered me to be completely delivered from
them—by His Spirit, not a superstition-based dream catcher
from a tribal shaman. He will do the same for your children!

First, we must define what a child's nightmare is. It is similar to how I defined nightmares earlier: a dream or vision that
causes fear, terror, panic and/or anxiety. Clinical studies have
shown that these dreams occur during REM sleep and often
include experiences of falling and being chased, bitten, frightened and eaten by monsters or animals. The dream carries a
threat of danger—in gray but sometimes very vivid colors—and
vivid activity that causes the child to wake up abruptly. It is

remembered after waking and often hinders the child's ability to go back to sleep.

Night terrors differ from dreams in that the child is not actively dreaming, as we understand it. He or she simply wakes up screaming or terrorized and disoriented; later the child cannot recall the dream that caused the terror. These usually occur earlier in the night, before the period of early morning when most dreams occur.

Whether nightmares or night terrors, these are uncomfortable experiences for our children and concerning to us as parents. Many times I have been approached by parents for help. In the past, I gave a pat answer: "Well . . . anoint them at night before they fall asleep and pray for God's protection." But, dear one, I have learned much over the years, and I have come to the conclusion that the Lord wants us to teach our children how to exercise their spiritual authority over fears, devilish assignments or any thought that might steal their godly inheritance as a victor in Christ. After all, they are children of the King. They have the same Holy Spirit in them that we have . . . which means they have authority over the enemy, just as we do!

I have also concluded that God is fully aware of the dreams our children have. He will use (*not cause*) night terrors and nightmares to equip our children to rise up, face their fears, speak to the devil and command him to flee from their night seasons.

So, parents, what should we look for as influences that cause these nightmares and night scares?

Unrepented Personal Sin

Ask your child if there is something she (or he) might have done that makes her feel ashamed or guilty. Be patient; it may take some time for your child to respond. Encourage her in the true meaning of repentance—in English, it means "regret and remorse." Your child might have deep feelings of regret, sadness or even disappointment that end up as nightmares in which she is deserving of punishment. Depending on their ages, children cannot necessarily process emotions any other way.

Your child might dream of his own pet chasing him and attempting to bite him; this might mean he believes he is shameful and deserves punishment from a God who is close but vengeful. It is possible the child is afraid of a parent's disapproval; therefore unconditional love needs to be expressed to him as he walks through understanding his dreams.

It is important to explain to your children that in the New Testament (such as in Matthew 4:17), repentance means a change of heart or a change of mind. It means to change the way we think about God and also about ourselves. Encourage your children to accept God's forgiveness and see themselves as children of God walking in spiritual authority over temptation and over the wiles of the devil.

Instruct your children *not* to be ashamed or discouraged—when they fall or fail, teach them to accept Christ's love and forgiveness and then get up and get back on track. Explain to your children that we walk out our salvation, continually taking our messes to the cross and giving them to Jesus. If you begin this at an early age, your children will live lives of limitless living! It is sad that I went through most of my life in shame only to realize later that God never held one single sin against me! You can lead your children into greater freedom as they express their dreams to you. And teach them that *you* love them for who they are and admire them for what they do (again—unconditional love).

Generational Sin

I have discussed generational sin already, but it is worth revisiting in the context of breaking off generational sins from our children. Numbers 14:18 discusses the origin of a generational curse: "The LORD is slow to anger, abounding in love and forgiving sin and rebellion. Yet he does not leave the guilty unpunished; he punishes the children for the sin of the fathers to the third and fourth generation."

I know it sounds unfair for the Lord to punish our children for the sins that we commit, but there is much more to understanding this passage properly. The English word *punish* in this passage is the Hebrew word *paqad*, meaning "to visit (with friendly or hostile intent), to oversee, muster, charge, care for, miss, deposit." It is true that when a father or mother lives an ungodly lifestyle, the children are likely to practice the same ungodly standard of living. An alcoholic father, for instance, is highly likely to have a child who later becomes an alcoholic. But we can trust God! Why? Because if there is a generational sin, God wants to punish that sinful influence—*not the person!* He promises to "visit" our children and charge them with purpose and to also "deposit" His character and holiness within them. How does He do this? Through their dreams and visions. If He reveals a sin through a divine visitation, He also brings with it the realization of the need for repentance. Once there is repentance of the sin, He supernaturally charges our children with power over the temptation of that sin.

The Lord desires to set our children free! They need us to explain generational sin to them—but in a way that they understand that *God reveals to always heal.*

Opportunities for Spiritual Promotion

God desires for each of us to grow in our spiritual authority—especially our children! I have discovered that if I have a nightmare and am being attacked and feel fearful, God uses the dream to give me an understanding that I need to rise up in authority over that fear. It took me many years to discover this valuable truth. Every nightmare offers us an opportunity to become an overcomer! We do not have to allow nightmares and terrorizing dreams to control us and our emotions any longer; rather, we can use these times as opportunities to mature in our godly authority and learn to overcome. As each of us overcomes, more authority is given, right? Well, it is the same with our children.

When my daughter was nearly eight, she had a dream that four snakes were chasing her down the street. She told me she found a shovel and started trying to whack at them. Finally they went back into the woods. It was not a week later that she had the same dream. In fact, it was repeated at least four or five more times.

I was teaching her Sunday school class at the time, and I remember teaching about using our spiritual authority and commanding the spirit of fear and the devil to leave. I had no idea that Kim used that teaching to deal with her dreams. In fact, she later told me that when she had the dream again, she actually reminded herself during the dream that she needed to rise up in authority and command the snakes to leave! She said this the way an eight-year-old would, of course. (I documented this in my dream journal at the time, and while rummaging through my many files of dreams, I ran across this one that Kim had. Thankfully, I had made a note that I was teaching on spiritual authority when Kim got the victory over that nightmare.)

Dear one, there is no doubt that God was teaching Kim how to use her spiritual authority. We each need to remind our children that no matter what our ages, we have all authority over the wicked one, especially the spirit of fear! By the way, Kim never had that dream again.

Lucid Dreaming

Nightmares do not have to continue to terrorize your precious children! In fact, nightmares and night scares can be very helpful in developing your children's spiritual maturity. How? Through a form of dreaming called *lucid dreaming*. I have also discussed this previously, but let me put it in the simplest terms so that you can easily relate it to your children's dreams. Lucid dreams are dreams in which you are completely aware that you are dreaming. When you awake from them, you can think about how to change the outcome of the dream, fall back asleep and actually control the dream! Lucid dreaming is a powerful tool that has been recognized since the nineteenth century; a Dutch psychiatrist and writer, Frederik van Eeden, coined the term in 1913. Dear one, please understand that this is not New Age, nor is it a type of mind control. It is simply part of the untapped potential in our brains that becomes available to us as our minds are renewed in Christ. Many Christian authors who are writing about dreams mention lucid dreaming.

Only recently has the general public been made aware of this gift from the Lord. And let me say that it works! Do you recall my lucid dream about the three Jezebels in my car? In the dream, I was driving my car, and three other women in it were causing confusion. They each possessed a controlling Jezebel spirit. I was miserable around them and wanted to get out of the car. Suddenly I awoke, and I pondered the dream for a few minutes as I lay in bed. I was talking to the Lord about those three women, and He said, *Why don't you just tell them to get out of your car?* So, I fell asleep back into the dream, and in the dream I commanded them and the Jezebel spirit to get out. And they did! ('Nuff said about that dream.)

Lucid dreaming is consciously interacting with people and events within a dream. It is one of the most powerful tools that the Lord has given us—and especially our children—to resist the bondage of fear that the devil tries to impose through nightmares. When children dream of being bullied at school, it is often a sign that it is actually happening or that they feel threatened in some way. We can teach them how to go back into the dream, face the fears and command them to go. We can teach them that when they know they are dreaming, they can consciously take authority in the dream. This does not mean action in the natural is not necessarily needed at school, but I am concentrating on the emotions, such as fear, that the situation produces.

I think it is sad that seminaries do not teach about lucid dreaming. Many have actually labeled it as New Age. But we have to look at *the motivation and the teacher*. If the motivation for teaching about lucid dreaming is to connect the child with God, to teach and impart methods of spiritual warfare and fulfill righteousness, then we know this is not New Age.

Think about it. When we, as adults, awake from nightmares, we are normally gripped with fear. Our children often run to the bedroom afraid and crying after experiencing nightmares. But we can calm them down, let them know they are safe, talk to them and encourage them to go back to bed. Tell them that when they go back to sleep, they should tell that fear and the origin of it to leave, thereby gaining a victory over torment and terror. Even better, teach your child how to plead the blood over the situation in the dream. With younger children, you may have to go back to their rooms with them to model what to do, especially at first. The day they understand that when they see a dark spirit, it actually means they have authority over it will be the beginning of their freedom!

Whatever you do, do not say, "It's just your imagination!" If they are told that, they will shut down and probably keep having nightmares . . . or not dream much at all anymore. Remember that every dream is an opportunity for us, and our children, to shift into a new beginning! For more information on children's lucid dreams, I highly recommend the book *Dreams, Children and the Night Season* by Recie Saunders (7 Spirits Production Co., 2015).

Dream Sharing with Our Children

Dream sharing with our children is a very unique vehicle for making contact with them—on the emotional level as well as the creative level. By sharing and exploring dreams together, we can discover meanings of images and stories of dreams that are vital in their hearts and minds. When a parent shares his/her dreams with the children, as appropriate, you might be surprised how very much they want to be involved in the discussion! When I shared my dreams with Kim, she would ask tons of questions, like she wanted to help me figure out the meanings of my dreams. Amazingly, she asked questions that at times caused me to pause . . . I suppose it was her childlike faith that quickened my spirit. Though she was young, she knew the Lord, and, as you know from Him visiting her in her dreams, He knew how to speak through her!

I am grateful that I listened to my daughter's dreams when she was a child. When adults treat their children's dreams as important and worthy of discussion, the children themselves begin to pay attention to them. But if dreams, especially nightmares, are treated as mere figments of the imagination, the result will be that children feel their experiences are insignificant. Telling your child, "Oh, it was just a dream," will hinder a child's emotional well-being. *Every child needs to be heard.* Not listening to them will result in children beginning to withdraw and isolate . . . feeling that their emotions and dreams are not noteworthy. If a parent will be patient, ask questions and encourage a child to recall the dream, the child will be more apt to communicate what goes on in his or her private world of dreams. Many dreams express feelings that are difficult for children to put into words, and, therefore, the parent becomes essential in helping discover the meanings of them.

A friend of mine—I will name him Michael in this book— shared with me that as a child he had many nightmares in which he was falling, stumbling around, being knocked around uncontrollably and losing control. Thirty years later, his son began to have similar dreams. The father talked to someone he knew who interpreted dreams. He found out that it was not uncommon for symbols to be passed on generationally, and so he attended a children's workshop on dreams, thinking that he could help himself and his child understand the dreams. In the workshop, the children were encouraged to draw pictures of their dreams. The father was encouraged to do the same and to draw the earliest memories of his dreams. Some of the parents grumbled a bit, but Michael was completely intrigued.

Childhood dreams are pregnant with all types of creativity and psychological possibilities. When Michael took different colors and began to draw, he was amazed at how many childhood memories returned. He began to draw rows of houses on different hillsides. Then he drew stones rolling down the streets, completely out of control. Michael's father was a prominent military officer and, as a result, was stationed in many different countries. Michael never knew permanency, was not able to establish solid relationships and felt as if he stumbled through school and life. He had "rolled uncontrollably" from house to house . . . all seemingly "downhill."

Michael was amazed how the metaphors in his dreams represented his innermost emotions, disappointments and fears as a child. As an adult, he realized the feelings were still there! Michael began to work through his dreams, forgiving his father for moving him around so often. He even turned down a promotion which would have required him to move his family around quite often. He decided he would not take a risk, even if he had to sacrifice a promotion, because he was concerned that his own son might feel tossed to and fro.

Michael began to talk to his son about his fears of feeling out of control. He found out that his son had overheard his father discussing a possible move, and the child did not want to be uprooted from his friends. Therefore, he intensely engaged in his son's dream again, discussed it and calmed his son's fears.

Teaching Your Child about Rescripting

Rescripting is a process in which you invite your children to use their imagination concerning the outcome of their dreams and guide them in doing so. The parent actually encourages the child to imagine changes in the dream by reenacting or rewriting the plot. By brainstorming an outcome together, the parent can help the child attach a positive conclusion to the dream. This is different from lucid dreaming in that it is more of a role play and a creative use of the imagination while completely awake. Rescripting is simply another way of creating a new ending to a dream. Children with nightmares can be taught to throw off the yoke of oppression from demonic dreams by acting like a well-known cartoon character, such as Spider-Man, who rescues the entire situation in the dream. Biblical examples of David defeating his Goliath and Samson gaining victory over the Philistines can also be used. This method of rescripting empowers the child's imagination and creativity. It causes the child to refocus on who he or she is in Christ, the promises of God and the faithfulness of God to protect His precious child. The understanding of identity and relationship with the Lord that comes through these playacting times can easily become integrated into a child's view of himself during a threatening or disturbing situation. And in later dreams the playacting helps reveal them as gaining victory over the crisis.

Though my daughter is not a small child any longer, I clearly remember our special times together at the playground, at the PlayPlace at McDonald's, at the city zoo and in the car to school and home. As a parent raising a child in a society full of pressures (even years ago there was pressure!), I found it difficult to spend quality time with her, so I tried to make the most of every moment we had. I loved her childlike expressions and communications. We would sing songs together, songs we knew and, at times, songs we made up as we drove down the road. We would sing about her dog and her other pets and deliberately make them funny so we could laugh together. I know now I was inviting her imagination into those songs and even allowing her dreams to be expressed. She eventually added her own imaginative words . . . and when she did, it was quite enlightening.

One day, we were singing about her poodle, Missy, while driving to school. Missy was an adorable pet—white and curly, a small ball of heavenly fluff. We trained Missy to sit in the rear basket of Kim's bicycle. When Kim was eight, we moved from our home in Lewisville, Texas, to a new neighborhood in Hurst, Texas. One day Kim took off with Missy in the back basket, and down the street they went, like two peas in a pod. Suddenly, Missy jumped out of the basket! She had never done that before. The only thing we could think of was that the neighborhood was unfamiliar and she was attempting to acclimate herself. When she leaped out, she was instantly struck by an oncoming car. Kim was devastated, of course. So was the driver of the car. And so were we, her parents.

For days Kim cried in her sleep. She began to have terrible nightmares. Kim would dream about the day she placed Missy in that basket, and somehow in the dream she would try to save Missy from death. In one dream, Kim jumped in front of the oncoming car and was run over herself—Missy lived, but Kim died. In other dreams, she would wake up in a terror, thinking that she must save Missy from that horrible accident. It was as if she wanted to go back into the dream and change the outcome. Though it was impossible to keep Missy from experiencing death in the natural, I now know that there are opportunities when dreaming to fall back asleep and take charge of the outcome of the dream. At the time this was occurring, however, I had no clue how to help Kim except to console her when she cried and listen to her as she discussed her dreams. Here is the story of Kim's "healed heart" the best way I can recall it:

One day on the way to school, Kim said, "Mom, I have a song."

"Really? That's great. Why don't you sing, and I'll join in."

And she went singing with joy in her heart: "I miss Missy . . . I miss my Missy. She is not dead . . . she lives forever in my heart! . . . She lives . . . she lives . . . forever in my heart." Then she looked at me and added, "Missy forgives me and I forgive her for leaving me. She lives forever in my heart."

I was stunned! *Missy forgives her?* What was that about? I told her, "Kim, I'm so glad Missy forgives you."

"Yes, Mom," she answered, "I dreamed about Missy last night. She was in heaven. I saw her in heaven and she ran up and licked me and was so happy to see me. I knew that she forgave me for putting her in my basket that day. And Missy looked right into my eyes, and I said, 'Missy, I forgive you for jumping out of the basket and leaving me.' Missy said, 'I will live forever in your heart.'"

Wow! I thought. *I need to draw on Kim's imagination some more and provide more positive memory.* (Keep in mind that I did not know that I was empowering Kim with rescripting.)

"Let's add to your song then, okay?" I encouraged her eagerly.

"Sure! Missy lives forever in my heart . . . in my heart . . . deep, deep down in my heart!"

Then I added to Kim's song. "In Kim's heart where Jesus also lives . . . where Jesus lives, too!"

Kim concluded, "Missy and Jesus . . . Missy and Jesus—" She stopped. "Mom! Jesus is now playing with Missy, and Missy is so happy. I'm so glad that Missy found Jesus and loves heaven."

I remember this occurrence well because it is written in my journal and is forever in my precious memories bank. But it was the last time we sang about Missy, cried about Missy or even mentioned Missy again. Kim's dream and her ability to imagine Missy beyond that horrible experience went into a place in her heart that was completely healed.

Welcoming the Dreams

The best way to guide your children with their dreams is to continually invite them to share them with you. Have an attitude, always, of welcoming your children's dreams. When you do this, it proves to them that you have an attitude of accepting any dream, no matter how short, confusing or terrifying it might be. Try to keep in mind that every dream, even the most bizarre ones, can be an avenue for emotional healing and creative exploration. By taking time to listen to their dreams, expressions and voice inflections, you will discover avenues that frighten them, excite them or hinder them emotionally. You will be amazed how you are able to build your child's self-esteem through their dreams!

Imagine, for example, that Johnny loves playing baseball, and he dreams of hitting a home run. You have limitless possibilities for preparing him for his next game! Obviously, a dream of hitting a home run would boost a child's confidence, but there is still "homework" to do, such as beefing up batting practice, working on making contact with the ball and, of course, giving Johnny all those "you can do it" pep talks. But if Johnny does not hit a home run during the next game? That is the opportunity to remind your child that being an athlete is not his true identity, and also that everyone makes mistakes, which is part of everyday life. Opportunities like these are profitable whenever we discuss being performance driven, for you can remind your child that winning the game is not nearly as important as playing and enjoying the sport. Whether Johnny hits a home run or not, the dream empowered Johnny with a hope and a goal, which every child needs—and the opportunity came thanks to his dream and your invitation to share it with you.

Being a curious, excited and welcoming parent will empower your child to feel comfortable sharing his dreams . . . even day-dreams. You will notice his dream life will be filled with joyful expectation and calming of fears. Do not put too much pressure on him, for he might stop sharing. Have fun with the symbolism, ask questions and invite his imagination into the exploration of his dreams. You will discover that the Lord will empower you as the adult to know how to pray and help your children with their dreams. Inspire your children to draw out their dreams, act out different characters in them and make rhymes about them. Have fun, but at the same time develop discernment along with a listening ear.

When guiding children through their dreams, parents need to keep in sight these important goals: to help them develop a relationship with God, maintain emotional stability and strengthen a rich capacity for creativity. As I have said, our children have the same Holy Spirit living in them as adults do! He will speak to them in symbols and parables, even literally at times, because He loves them and desires that each of them fulfill their destinies.

Let me make a very strong suggestion to you, as a parent, who desires to provide the very best support for them to experience a successful life, fulfill divine destiny and experience life to the fullest: *Look to their dreams!* Dreams are free. You do not have to travel far to find them, they do not cost you money and they never need batteries! Dreams from God can take them places they have never seen and give details they can further explore on the web, in magazines, in dictionaries, etc. God can download witty inventions in a dream, skill sets for chess, designs for building airplanes, dress patterns for a fashion designer . . . He is an unlimited God. And He takes the limits off in our children's dreams. All you need is a bit of patience and a sense of childlike curiosity and adventure, and off you go!

Remember, children will remember more clearly the vivid details of a nightmare rather than other dreams. This is because nightmares awaken them abruptly and dramatically. Even so, studies prove that the majority of our children's dreams are of creativity, playfulness, adventure and power. When adults learn to cultivate the details, images and concepts within their dreams, it empowers them to think more positively and creatively—like taking off all limitations and releasing them to greater levels of productivity and unexplored innovation. Yes, your child may be an inventor, an author, an artist, an actor, a teacher, a minister of the Gospel, just waiting to be unleashed!

Dear one, God is faithful. He will pursue your children through dreams and visions so that they fulfill divine destiny. The very best is yet ahead! Remember, every dream is a mystery waiting to be discovered and revealed. So pray, seek understanding, search and find the answers that unlock the doors of fulfillment, encouragement, success and completeness in Christ . . . for *both* you and your children!

Reflection Concerning Your Children

- Does your child have fear? Most children do—some more than others. But the Word states that fear is not from God. In fact, fear brings torment. Take a moment to recall a dream or nightmare that your child has shared. Then, guide your child in rescripting. Tell him or her to use imagination concerning the outcome. Ask your child to role-play with an entirely new ending. Do this every day for one week. Document below if the child has a similar type of dream with a victorious outcome.

- Give the Lord praise every day for speaking to your children through dreams and visions!

Notes

Chapter 1: Meet the Master Potter

1. James W. Goll and Michal Ann Goll, *Dream Language: The Power of Dreams, Revelations, and the Spirit of Wisdom* (Shippensburg, Pa.: Destiny Image, 2006), 20.
2. Marilyn Hickey, *The Names of God* (New Kensington, Pa.: Whitaker House, 2009), Kindle edition, chapter 15.

Chapter 5: Dreams That Influence Our Destiny

1. Sandie Freed, *Breaking the Threefold Demonic Cord: How to Discern and Defeat the Lies of Jezebel, Athaliah and Delilah* (Grand Rapids, Mich.: Chosen, 2008), 53. I have written much more on the python spirit in this book.

Chapter 6: Other Common Destiny Dreams

1. Chuck D. Pierce and Rebecca Wagner Sytsema, *When God Speaks: How to Interpret Dreams, Visions, Signs and Wonders* (Minneapolis: Chosen, 2015), 80–81.
2. Jane Hamon, *Dreams and Visions: Understanding and Interpreting God's Messages to You* (Minneapolis: Chosen, 2016), 50.

Bibliography

I would like to give credit to the many different people who have written books that I have read, or whom I have studied under and honor as mentors in my own personal journey of dream interpretation. The list of dream symbols and interpretations that I provided in chapter 9 is composed from my own personal revelation given by the Holy Spirit and from the following references.

Breathitt, Barbie L. *Dream Encounters: Seeing Your Destiny from God's Perspective*. North Richland Hills, Tex.: Barbie Breathitt Enterprises, LLC, 2009.

Goll, James W. and Michal Ann Goll. *Dream Language: The Prophetic Power of Dreams, Revelations and the Spirit of Wisdom*. Shippensburg, Pa.: Destiny Image, 2006.

Hamon, Jane. *Dreams and Visions: Understanding and Interpreting God's Messages to You*. Minneapolis: Chosen, 2016.

Ibojie, Joe. *Illustrated Dictionary of Dream Symbols*. San Giovanni Teatino, Italy: Destiny Image Europe, 2005.

Milligan, Ira. *Understanding the Dreams You Dream*. Shippensburg, Pa.: Destiny Image, 2010.

Nelson, Jerame. *Activating Your Dream Language: A Closer Look at Understanding the Realm of Dreams and Visions*. San Diego: Living at His Feet Ministries, 2012.

Pierce, Chuck D. *When God Speaks: How to Interpret Dreams, Visions, Signs and Wonders*. Minneapolis: Chosen, 2005. (Originally published Ventura, Calif.: Regal, 2005.)

Smith, Laura Harris. *Seeing the Voice of God: What God is Telling You through Dreams and Visions*. Minneapolis: Chosen, 2014.

Wolfe, Tyler. *Biblical Dream Symbols Dictionary*. 2nd ed. Vern Tyler Wolf, 2013.

Index

Sandie Freed is an internationally recognized speaker and author of more than thirteen books. Known as one who has been "freed" to become a freedom fighter, her passion is to empower others to experience freedom in Christ. Sandie's goal in both writing and ministering is to teach the Word of God with power and demonstration, so that each of God's children experiences life and transformation. Sandie always speaks from her heart, and her revelation and transparency captivate hearts to shift into divine purpose. She releases a powerful anointing of healing and hope to those who have been held captive. With a strong anointing in discerning of spirits, Sandie has been known to discern territorial strongholds and release churches and regions from spiritual assignments that withhold finances, deliverance and breakthroughs. She is also known for her cutting-edge prophetic ministry, and she moves strongly in words of knowledge and realms of the supernatural.

As a modern-day Joseph in the area of dream interpretation, Sandie has become particularly anointed in releasing and activating dreams and visions, as well as in dream interpretation. She has been featured numerous times on various radio broadcasts and television programs, such as Daystar's *Celebration* with Marcus and Joni Lamb, *Life Today* with James Robison, and the CornerStone Network with Donald Black. Sandie and her husband, Mickey, are ordained by Bishop Bill Hamon (Christian International Ministries) and serve on his board of governors. Presently they pastor Lifegate Church International in Hurst, Texas. They have been married since 1973 and have one daughter, Kimberly, a son-in-law, Daniel Wheeler, and two wonderful grandsons, Elijah and Perrin Wheeler.